Making Peace with Referendums

I0891877

Syracuse Studies on Peace and Conflict Resolution
Robert A. Rubinstein and Çerağ Esra Çuhadar, *Series Editors*

SELECT TITLES FROM SYRACUSE STUDIES ON PEACE AND CONFLICT RESOLUTION

Back Channel Negotiation: Secrecy in the Middle East Peace Process
Anthony Wanis-St. John

Civil Society, Conflict Resolution, and Democracy in Nigeria
Darren Kew

Democracy and Conflict Resolution: The Dilemmas of Israel's Peacemaking
Miriam Fendius Elman, Oded Haklai, and Hendrik Spruyt, eds.

Exploring the Power of Nonviolence: Peace, Politics, and Practice
Randall Amster and Elavie Ndura, eds.

Globalization, Social Movements, and Peacebuilding
Jackie Smith and Ernesto Verdeja, eds.

Jerusalem: Conflict and Cooperation in a Contested City
Madelaine Adelman and Miriam Fendius Elman, eds.

Peacekeeping in South Lebanon: Credibility and Cooperation
Vanessa Newby

Youth Encounter Programs in Israel: Pedagogy, Identity, and Social Change
Karen Ross

For a full list of titles in this series, visit https://press.syr.edu/supressbook-series/syracuse-studies-on-peace-and-conflict-resolution.

Making Peace with Referendums

Cyprus and Northern Ireland

Joana Amaral

Syracuse University Press

The research presented in this book was funded by the Portuguese Science and Technology Foundation (FCT).

Syracuse, New York 13244-5290

First Edition 2019
19 20 21 22 23 24   6 5 4 3 2 1

∞ The paper used in this publication meets the minimum requirements of the American National Standard for Information Sciences—Permanence of Paper for Printed Library Materials, ANSI Z39.48-1992.

For a listing of books published and distributed by Syracuse University Press, visit www.SyracuseUniversityPress.syr.edu.

ISBN: 978-0-8156-3624-3 (hardcover)   978-0-8156-3642-7 (paperback)
978-0-8156-5470-4 (e-book)

Library of Congress Cataloging-in-Publication Data
Names: Amaral, Joana, author.
Title: Making peace with referendums : Cyprus and Northern Ireland / Joana Amaral
Description: Syracuse, New York : Syracuse University Press, 2019. | Series: Syracuse studies on peace and conflict resolution | Includes bibliographical references and index. |
Identifiers: LCCN 2019000811 (print) | LCCN 2019011551 (ebook) | ISBN 9780815654704 (E-book) | ISBN 9780815636243 (hardcover : alk. paper) | ISBN 9780815636427 (pbk. : alk. paper)
Subjects: LCSH: Peace-building—Case studies. | Referendum—Case studies. | Peace-building—Cyprus. | Peace-building—Northern Ireland. | Referendum—Cyprus. | Referendum—Northern Ireland. | Cyprus—History—Cyprus Crisis, 1974– | Northern Ireland—Politics and government—1968–1998.
Classification: LCC JZ5538 (ebook) | LCC JZ5538 .A428 2019 (print) | DDC 941.60824—dc23
LC record available at https://lccn.loc.gov/2019000811

Manufactured in the United States of America

Peace treaties do not make peace; people make peace.

—Harold H. Saunders

Contents

Preface *ix*
Acknowledgments *xv*
Abbreviations *xvii*

1. Peace Negotiations and Peace Agreement Referendums *1*
2. How Peace Negotiations Shape Agreement Referendums *16*
3. The Case Studies *31*
4. The Annan Plan Experience in Cyprus *50*
5. The Good Friday Agreement Experience in Northern Ireland *78*
6. Comparing the Cypriot and Northern Irish Experiences *104*
7. A New Paradigm in Peace Negotiations *122*

Conclusion *137*

Bibliography *145*
Index *169*

Preface

REFERENDUMS ARE STEADILY becoming a vital feature of contemporary peacemaking. Among the varied purposes for which they are held in peace processes, referendums have become an important, and perhaps necessary, source of legitimacy for the ratification of peace agreements, but with mixed results. The two cases compared in this book are paradigmatic in their opposing outcomes and consequences. In May 1998, the victory of the "yes" vote in the Good Friday Agreement (GFA)[1] referendum in Northern Ireland was a critical turning point in the transformation of a conflict that had lingered for decades between the Nationalist and Unionist communities. A few years later, in April 2004, the Annan Plan referendum in Cyprus was its antithesis. The agreement aimed at allowing the island to become a European Union (EU) member as a united country but failed to receive the support of the Greek Cypriot community, while the majority of the voters in the Turkish Cypriot community supported it.

Unfortunately, more often than not, peace agreements are rejected by popular vote despite strenuous political negotiations. Although referendums are increasingly used in peace

1. The Northern Ireland peace agreement is also referred to as Belfast Agreement. For simplicity, it is referred to as "Good Friday Agreement" or "GFA" throughout this book.

processes, we know little about how to get peace agreements supported in referendums. The study of peace referendums itself is relatively recent, as is the use of referendums in peace processes. The broader research and theory on peace negotiations and mediation has traditionally focused on uncovering how the process of negotiating peace helps political leaders reduce military tensions, improve relationships, and come to different types of agreements, but not to successful agreement referendums. Research on referendums typically studies voting behaviors using public opinion polls and surveys or analyzing referendum campaigns, seldom considering how negotiation processes shape them.

By bridging the literatures on peace negotiations and the broad literature on referendums, this book takes advantage of the knowledge from both fields to answer the question: Do peace negotiations shape peace agreement referendums? And if so, how? It essentially sets out to discover if the way peace agreements are negotiated has an influence on whether they are supported in a referendum. This is achieved through an in-depth study of whether and how the Annan Plan and GFA negotiations shaped their respective agreement referendums, and a comparison of the two cases. For the first time, referendum results are studied here as a crucial outcome of contemporary peace negotiation processes with the underlying aim of uncovering how peace negotiations can favor broad support for peace agreements and avoid their rejection in the polls.

Although the Annan Plan and Good Friday Agreement are selected primarily because one agreement was accepted and the other not, I also look at the percentages of support from the main local communities in each case. Especially in peace agreement referendums, it is important that the agreement be supported by each of the communities involved. Arguably, when differences in community support are better understood, we will be able to set up a less polarizing and more successful referendum experience. Therefore, this study investigates not only how the Annan Plan and the Good Friday Agreement negotiations led to different referendum outcomes but also how the negotiations themselves shaped the differences in support between and across the communities.

This book begins by identifying the gap in academic research and literature between existing knowledge on peace negotiations and that on referendums. Although the outcome of a peace agreement referendum can have a profound impact on a peace process, the literature on peace negotiations has not yet considered this a significant outcome of a negotiation process. I review the evolving notion of what outcomes are produced by negotiation processes in conflict contexts and show the limitations of existing studies on peace referendums. In doing so, agreement referendum results are put forward as a new crucial determinant of the success or failure of contemporary peace negotiations. After all, negotiations that fail to produce an agreement that receives support in a referendum can hardly be considered successful. I then turn to the wider literature on referendums. The most extensive studies on referendums have been in the context of European integration. I present a review of this literature in order to understand what influences voting behaviors in referendums. The emerging understanding is then applied to the study of peace referendums in the rest of the book. Bridging existing knowledge of peace negotiations and referendums, I create a research design that allows a qualitative study of the impact of negotiation process characteristics on referendum outcomes, namely, by studying if and how they shaped the following: political parties' support for the agreement in the referendum, the organization and strength of the campaigns, and voter information and uncertainty.

The Annan Plan and GFA negotiations and referendums are first analyzed individually in chapters four and five. The presentation of the cases does not follow a chronological order—I begin with the Cypriot case. Instead, the structure respects the order in which the case study research was conducted. In both case study analyses, I show how mediation strategies, political inclusion, civil society inclusion, and agreement design influenced the referendum results by showing their impact on any of the three referendum outcome determinants: political party support for the agreement, the composition and strength of the "yes" and "no" referendum campaigns, and the information available to the public on the issues at stake in the referendum, namely the content of the peace agreement. I compare the findings of the two cases in chapter 6 and discuss policy implications in the final chapter. Even though the chapters analyze each of the negotiation process variables independently, it is not meant to suggest that each has an independent impact on the referendum outcome. As will become evident, significant interactions between these variables shaped the referendum results. Importantly, there is no intention to claim that only these particular characteristics of the negotiation process shaped the referendum outcomes, since factors outside the negotiations were also key. Rather, it is to test if and how these specific aspects had a significant influence.

To uncover the linkages between the negotiation and referendum experiences, this book draws on a wide range of firsthand accounts from political leaders and representatives of civil society groups who either participated in the negotiations or the referendum campaigns, as well as academic experts and journalists. The information needed for this research could only be provided by those directly involved in the negotiation processes and referendum campaigns, including what shaped their personal and their parties' positioning in the referendum and/or their campaign activities. Referendum campaigners' personal accounts were essential to uncovering if and how negotiation process conditions influenced the organization and strength of the campaigns they led. In addition, I used official documents, memoirs, and media reports, especially to triangulate interview data.

The interview material was collected in semistructured face-to-face and telephone interviews conducted in Cyprus and Northern Ireland in 2014. To assure the comparability of the data, I used the same semistructured interview scripts in both case studies. Politicians taking part in negotiations were asked about what impacted their personal and their parties' positioning in the referendum and their campaigning activities. More in-depth and targeted questions explored the impact of negotiation process characteristics. I also interviewed politicians from political parties who did not directly participate in the negotiations. Their testimony was relevant because their parties campaigned for a certain referendum result, and I wanted to know if they were included in the negotiations in any unofficial capacity.

I used a snowballing process to select other individuals and representatives of groups involved in the referendum process. The aim was to gain access to those who were most active in the referendum campaigns. By doing this, I could ensure that the "field" informed the research on potential sources of information and interview subjects. Accordingly, I selected representatives of civil society and NGOs, as well as individuals active in the "yes" and "no" campaigns, to interview. They were also asked if and how negotiating conditions influenced the organization and strength of the referendum campaigns they led. More specifically, they were asked what helped or constricted their ability to develop their campaigning activities and to organize and mobilize people. I also asked civil society actors about their possible involvement in the negotiation process.

I interviewed journalists who reported on the negotiations and referendums for two reasons. First, to be able to compare journalists' access to information on the negotiations in each of the cases. Second, as the media play a significant role in informing the public and shaping opinion, it was important to consider their impact. Finally, I interviewed academics and other officials, including members of the UN Good Offices Mission in Cyprus, for their expertise.

Although the Cypriot and Northern Irish peace negotiations have been extensively researched, by analyzing the two negotiation processes with a view to understanding how they shaped the referendum campaign period, this book casts a new light on key features of the peace negotiations. I analyze characteristics of the negotiations that are novel to existing literature on the two case studies, looking at the political inclusivity of the Annan Plan negotiations and the secrecy of the Multi-Party Talks in Northern Ireland, which have not been analyzed before.

The Cypriot and Northern Irish experiences, as recounted in this book, will show that peace referendums are deeply shaped by the negotiation process that precedes them and that, when referendums are used to seal a peace agreement, the negotiation process needs to adapt to that reality from the start. As an increasingly important feature of contemporary peace process, referendums bring important new challenges to peace negotiations. These challenges may well require a change of paradigm in the way peace negotiations are conducted and studied.

Acknowledgments

I WOULD LIKE TO EXPRESS my gratitude to Professor Neophytos Loizides and Professor Feargal Cochrane for inspiring and guiding the research I conducted for this book. Thank you to all those who read its several versions, especially Professor Anthony Wanis-St. John and Dr. Harmonie Toros, who provided insightful comments and encouragement. Thank you to the Centre for Conflict Studies at the University of Marburg for hosting me during the full course of this research and especially to Professor Thorsten Bonacker for his constant support. Thank you also to the Peace Research Institute Oslo (PRIO) Cyprus Centre and the Institute for the Study of Conflict Transformation and Social Justice at Queen's University Belfast for granting me access to their research facilities and allowing me to join their teams. Thank you to the Press and Information Office of the Ministry of Interior of the Republic of Cyprus for supporting my fieldwork in Cyprus and to the Cyprus Academic Dialogue for so warmly welcoming me into the association.

Thank you to Christoforos Fokaides, Quintin Oliver, Allan Leonard, Andri Prodromou, Evren Inancoglu, and many others for facilitating the first contact with several of the persons I interviewed for this research. Thank you also to Elizabeth Thompson for her editing work and Stephen Foose for his help proofreading.

Above all, thank you to all those in Cyprus and Northern Ireland who so kindly accepted my request for an interview back in 2014. It would have been impossible to write this book without your generous contributions. I am deeply grateful and appreciative of your willingness to share your experiences and opinions with me.

Abbreviations

AKEL	Progressive Party of the Working People (Greek: Anorthotikó Kómma Ergazómenou Laoú)
BBC	British Broadcasting Corporation
CTP	Republican Turkish Party (Turkish: Cumhuriyetçi Türk Partisi)
DIKO	Democratic Party (Greek: Dimokratikó Kómma)
DISY	Democratic Rally (Greek: Dimokratikós Synagermós)
DP	Democratic Party (Turkish: Demokrat Parti)
DUP	Democratic Unionist Party
EC	European Community
ECOWAS	Economic Community of West African States
EDEK	Movement for Social Democracy (Greek: Kinhma Sosialdimokraton)
EDI	United Democrats (Greek: Enomenoi Dimokrates)
EU	European Union
FARC	Revolutionary Armed Forces of Colombia (Spanish: Fuerzas Armadas Revolucionarias de Colombia)
GFA	Good Friday Agreement
KTOS	Turkish Cypriot Teachers Union (Turkish: Kibris Turk Ogretmenler Sendikasi)
NGO	Nongovernmental Organization
NICVA	Northern Ireland Council for Voluntary Action
NIWC	Northern Ireland Women's Coalition
PIRA	Provisional Irish Republican Army
PUP	Progressive Unionist Party
RUC	Royal Ulster Constabulary

SDLP	Social Democratic and Labour Party
TRNC	Turkish Republic of Northern Cyprus
UBP	National Unity Party (Turkish: Ulusal Birlik Partisi)
UDP	Ulster Democratic Party
UKUP	United Kingdom Unionist Party
UN	United Nations
UNFICYP	United Nations Peacekeeping Force in Cyprus
UUP	Ulster Unionist Party

Making Peace with Referendums

1

Peace Negotiations and Peace Agreement Referendums

What is an Outcome?

The understanding and definition of what is an outcome of a peace negotiation or mediation process has evolved over time. The study of these outcomes has broadened from an initial focus on tangible outcomes, such as cease-fires and other kinds of agreements, to more intangible outcomes, such as tension reduction or the improvement of the relationships between the parties in conflict. In this chapter, I expand the meaning to include peace agreement referendums.

The definition of an outcome of peace negotiations remains an open debate in international mediation literature (Bercovitch, Anagnoson, and Wille 1991; Bercovitch and Derouen 2004; Bercovitch 2006). In its most narrow definition, the outcome of a mediation process is any type of agreement reached between the negotiating parties. Researchers inadvertently defined this in the 1980s and 1990s when they began to ask why some negotiations succeeded while others failed. One of the first and most renowned mediation scholars, Jacob Bercovitch (1986; Bercovitch, Anagnoson, and Wille 1991) applied quantitative methods to determine which characteristics of a mediation process were associated with "successful" outcomes, defined and coded as the observance of a cease-fire, a partial settlement, or a full settlement. This tied the definition of "successful" or "effective" mediation early on in the emergence of the field to the need for measurable data. Yet as Bercovitch (2006, 301) himself later noted, as difficult and ongoing civil wars and ethnic conflicts continued to challenge diplomatic missions throughout the world, mediation scholars began to understand that mediation needed to affect the antagonist and mistrustful relationships between the parties in conflict, and not only focus on achieving agreements.

Negotiations between the highly antagonized parties in violent ethnic conflicts showed that not only is it more unlikely that negotiating parties will arrive at any sort of agreement, but also, even if they do, this is not sine qua non to it being implemented. Angola's civil war re-escalation after the Bicesse and Lusaka agreements of 1994[1], along with numerous other agreement implementation failures, including Sri Lanka in 1989, Somalia in 1993, Rwanda in 1994, and Sierra Leone in 1998 (Stedman 2001, 12), pushed scholars to take a longer-term perspective on outcomes. Some began to ask what makes an agreement "stick" or to consider its "durability." This opened up the field to the study of political leaders' negotiating behaviors, particularly how domestic conditions influence their ability to commit to an agreement (Haass 1991; Stedman 1991).

1. The Bicesse (1991) and Lusaka (1994) Agreements aimed at ending a two-decade civil war in Angola between the Marxist Popular Movement for the Liberation of Angola (MPLA) and the Union for the Total Independence of Angola (UNITA), but broke down after the UNITA leader, Jonas Savimbi, refused to accept defeat in the postagreement elections and re-escalated the conflict. The mediation process led by Portugal, the United States, Russia (the Troika), and the United Nations has been criticized for failing to put transitory institutions and rules in place to guarantee the country's transition into democracy (Messiant 2004, 18).

In quantitative studies, durability was conceptualized as the nonreoccurrence of violence during a given period after an agreement is reached. Some found that the offer of security guarantees by third parties was associated with more stable agreements after civil wars (Hartzell, Hoddie, and Rothchild 2001; Pearson et al. 2006, 121). Others showed mediated negotiation processes were likely to produce settlements that would break down within weeks of being agreed upon, unless they were supported by a peacekeeping operation and/or followed by a period of economic development (Quinn, Mason, and Gurses 2007, 189). Still others found that agreements containing provisions for the territorial autonomy of threatened groups (Hartzell, Hoddie, and Rothchild 2001, 202) and power-sharing provisions (Hartzell and Hoddie 2003), particularly on military and territorial issues (Jarstad and Nilsson 2008), were more likely to lead to a durable peace. This area of research looks beyond a simple bivariate outcome of an agreement having been reached or not to consider its "quality," although peace agreements remain the outcome of interest.

The burgeoning awareness that the arrival and implementation of an agreement requires a certain degree of trust between disputants drew scholars' attention to relational and more subjective negotiation outcomes (Kriesberg 2001; Bercovitch 2006). Studies emerged on conflicts with "enduring rivalries" where the prolonged experience of conflict further antagonized all parties and severely reduced the likelihood of an agreement being reached, let alone implemented. In such cases, it was argued, it was necessary to consider that the ability to reduce violent interactions between disputants was an important mediation outcome (Andersen et al. 2001; Greig 2001). These arguments take a step back from a *conflict resolution* focus and suggest the need to consider successful *conflict management* as a significant outcome. In such thinking, a mediation process's ability to be an alternative to armed conflict in protracted contexts and to keep the parties at the table is a considerable achievement in its own right.

The field of peace studies also contended with changes in the understanding of the limits of mediation. As peace scholars began the search for a definition and the components of peace, peace negotiations were understood as part of a broader peace process that takes place within societies. Concurrent with the development of critical theory, the opening up of the field to this larger political and sociological context invited criticism of the "elitist" approach hitherto dominating the practice and theory of peace negotiations and mediation (Burton 1987; Väyrynen 1991; Lederach 1997; Kaldor 2000; Byrne 2001; Ron 2009; Papagianni 2010). Peacebuilding scholars criticized peacemaking processes for being secretive and exclusionist and their consequent tendency to produce agreements accommodating the interests of political elites while failing to address the wider societal conflict. Such agreements are doomed to fail. Long-term peace, it is understood, is achieved by empowering and mobilizing local people to reframe their zero-sum and adversarial relationships into new and constructive ones (Lederach 1997).

The study of peace negotiations has expanded in recent years to include awareness of the need for societal transformation for peace to be sustainable. The important role other actors beyond political elites play in this process has been pivotal to this thinking. Recent research has found that the inclusion of civil society in the negotiation process has a positive impact on the sustainability of peace (Nilsson 2012). Having civil society actively engaged in a peace process is associated with peace agreements that are perceived as more balanced and legitimate, and more successfully implemented and durable. In addition to the inclusion of other actors, the use of participatory mechanisms and public diplomacy in peace negotiations has been found to favor greater public engagement with the peace process (Handelman 2012). Examples include the public consultation process in Colombia (Herbolzheimer 2016, 8) and the use of public opinion polling, or "peace polls," in Northern Ireland (Irwin 1999) and, more recently, in Cyprus (Interpeace 2014). Referendums have also been found to serve conflict resolution by signifying popular approval for peace processes, reducing democratic deficits in conflict settings, and encouraging civic engagement in political life (Haskell 2001; Lee and Mac Ginty 2012). Given their promise, recent studies have begun to ask how peace referendums aid or hinder peace processes (Lordos 2009; Kaymak 2012; Lee and Mac Ginty 2012; Loizides 2014; Qvortrup 2014). Peace negotiations, therefore, far from being an isolated affair between political elites, are beginning to be understood as playing a crucial role in reconciling societies by stimulating the wider public's interest, support, and involvement in creating their own peace (Cochrane 2000; Byrne 2001; Papagianni 2010).

Despite the growing understanding that public diplomacy plays a crucial role in managing public opinion during negotiation processes, the study of referendums in peace processes is far from sufficiently researched and theorized in conflict negotiation and mediation literature. The existing body of literature is typically based on case studies(Strauss 1993; Rynhold and Cohen 2003; Lordos 2009; Lee and Mac Ginty 2012; Somerville and Kirby 2012; Loizides 2014; Morgan-Jones, Loizides, and Stefanovic 2015), with the exception of Qvortrup's (2012; 2014) broader work on all types of referendums. Although some recommendations are made on how referendums can best be used in the context of peacemaking (Rynhold and Cohen 2003; Johansson 2009; Lee and Mac Ginty 2012; Loizides 2014, 2015), studies that aim specifically at understanding how referendums are shaped by peace negotiation processes are negligible. All the while, peace agreement referendums can be spectacular failures if the agreement reached by the representatives of the communities in conflict fails to gain the acceptance of the communities they purport to represent. The referendum on the Annan Plan in Cyprus and the referendum on the 2016 peace agreement between the Colombian government and the Revolutionary Armed Forces of Colombia (FARC) are two recent examples of this.

The success or failure of peace negotiations has traditionally been measured in terms of the outcomes of the bargaining process, and this, as noted above, typically takes place between political elites and excludes the people. Consequently, while the fate of an agreement in a referendum can dictate the success or failure of peace negotiations, scholars have not yet considered peace agreement referendum results as an outcome of the negotiation process, nor a measure of its success.

Peace Referendums

Referendums have been used to address political and ethnic conflicts for centuries (Qvortrup 2012; 2014), but have only recently begun to be used as tool of conflict resolution in contemporary peace processes. When used in conflict settings to further conflict resolution, referendums have a set of aims and challenges that merits their study as a distinct category within the universe of all types of referendums. I define peace referendums, or peacemaking referendums, as those referendums held to further an existing peacemaking process, which, therefore, ask the public about matters related, or relevant to, an existing negotiation/mediation process.

The issues that peace referendums address are typically related to power-sharing, self-determination, and territory. For example, the referendums in East Timor in 1999 and South Sudan in 2011 were used to determine the political status of a disputed territory. The South African referendum of 1992, on the other hand, aimed at getting the white community's endorsement of President F. W. de Klerk's negotiating position, particularly on the issue of the end of apartheid. These "mandate referendums," (Loizides 2015) allow political leaders to gain legitimacy and credibility for their position at the negotiations table. This can advance negotiations by increasing political leaders' accountability for commitments and concessions and avoid public opinion reversals down the line, while providing greater legitimacy to the peace negotiation process.

The use of referendums in peacemaking has increasingly served to ratify negotiated agreements, such as in Northern Ireland in 1998, Guatemala in 1999, Rwanda in 2003, Cyprus in 2004, Iraq in 2005, and Colombia in 2016. Peace agreement referendums can draw public[2] support for the implementation of an agreement, ripen negotiations by functioning as a deadline (Loizides 2014, 2015; Haskell 2001), and symbolise an important transitional point from conflict to peace (Lee and Mac Ginty 2012). Conversely, the rejection of a peace agreement can have serious consequences. The rejection of the Indigenous Rights Accords in Guatemala in 1999 and the rejection of the Annan Plan in Cyprus in 2004 brought these two peace processes to a standstill. In Colombia, a postreferendum parliamentary vote allowed the agreement to be implemented, but not without damaging consequences to the peace process.

The wider literature on other types of referendums suggests other possible advantages of referendums for peace processes. The referendum experience itself has the potential to reshape domestic politics by stimulating public and political debate on particular issues, building awareness, and educating citizens (Smith and Tolbert 2009). For example, Scranton

2. The "public" refers to the ordinary citizens of the communities who do not participate directly in the negotiation process, although its process and outcomes concern them.

(1993) argues that although the referendum in Panama in 1992 put to the vote a US-imposed constitution, the referendum encouraged Panamanian political leaders to work within a democratic process and to build democratic habits and institutions. In the Czech Republic, participation in pre-accession negotiations and the subsequent integration referendum in 2003 informed public debates, views, and opinions in favor of Europeanization (Baun et al. 2006, 250, 274). Referendums can also be undemocratic experiences, however. Their result can be manipulated through, for example, the way the question in the ballot is posed, the selection of the electorate, and voter coercion in the worst cases. The referendum on the status of the Ukrainian province of Crimea in March 2014, which saw an overwhelming majority of voters support its annexation to the Russian Federation, raised some of these issues. The Russian government's involvement in setting up the referendum and the circumstances under which the referendum was held have raised questions of the legality and legitimacy of the process and its result is not recognized internationally (Biersack and O'Lear 2014; Burke-White 2014).

To hold a referendum in a peace process presents considerable and unique challenges. First, the design of a referendum can be contentious. The UN-mediated negotiations in Western Sahara have stalemated for over two decades on the issue of who should be allowed to vote in a self-determination referendum (Solà-Martín 2007). Negotiations on a solution to the conflict in Nagorno-Karabakh have stalled over the issue of whether displaced Azerbaijani people should be able to participate in a status referendum (Johansson 2009, 123). Referendums may even exacerbate conflict and lead to violence escalation in the short term. This was the case in East Timor in 1999. Following a referendum where an overwhelming majority voted in favor of independence for the former Indonesian province, pro-independence voters were violently pursued by Indonesian government-supported militias. The international community (the UN and the Australian government in particular) has been heavily criticized for not having created the necessary security conditions for the referendum and its aftermath (Cotton 2007; see Wheeler & Dunne [2001] for a counter argument).

Critics of the use of referendums in peace processes argue that the referendum experience can become a source of rivalry, with the referendum result regarded as simply another conflict-like win-lose situation. Referendum campaigns may provide incentives for political leaders and other groups to mobilize support for their voting preferences by appealing to the very insecurities that caused the conflict in the first place (Reilly 2008, 233). As populist leaders or hardliners inflame public debate, the referendum campaign can become focused on divisive issues and further radicalize public opinion. Mac Ginty (2003) asserts that constitutional referendums—typical of peace agreement referendums—are unsuitable for ethnonational conflicts because they tend to present zero-sum choices around which ethnic differences can be reignited. The dichotomous either/or, yes/no nature of voting choices can have a negative impact in conflict contexts, polarizing already divided societies by creating referendum "winners" and "losers."

Given that the outcome of the referendum has such high stakes for a peace process, and especially considering it can reignite the conflict, it becomes crucial to understand whether and how the negotiation process itself can shape a referendum experience and result. I will return to the arguments for and against the use of referendums in peace processes in a later chapter of this book.

Referendum Outcomes

If the literature on peace referendums is scarce, the broader literature on referendums is vast, with a large body of work focusing on voting behaviors in European Union integration referendums. This particular literature is especially relevant to the study of peace referendums, as it examines cases of elite negotiated treaties ratified by a domestic referendum vote. Moreover, the two cases studied here, Northern Ireland and Cyprus, are in this geographical region. Turning to this wider literature to clarify what shapes a referendum outcome, I find three interrelated factors: the political parties' positions on the referendum; the composition and strength of the referendum campaigns; and voter information and uncertainty about the issues at stake in the referendum or the content of an agreement. I later use these three factors to build the research design for the study of the Northern Irish and Cypriot cases.

Political Party Support and Voter Alignment

Typically, politicians publicly support a specific position on the issue or issues at stake in the referendum. Whether independently or under the structure of their political party, they usually campaign in favor of one of the choices on the referendum ballot. For example, peace agreement referendums typically ask voters whether they support or do not support the implementation of the agreement and give them a choice of "yes" or "no."

Both quantitative and qualitative case study–based research finds political parties' preferences have significantly influenced European Union integration referendum results (Pierce, Valen, Henry, and Listhaug 1983, 61; Hobolt 2006, 641; Baun et al. 2006, 275; Lubbers 2008, 81). Political leaders are, in many instances, the most important source of information for voters on the referendum issues (Leduc 2002, 722). In fact, when in government, they may be constitutionally obligated to inform citizens about what is at stake in the referendum. In any case, political elites have considerable power to influence how voters perceive the question(s) asked in a referendum and how they frame the choices and their consequences (Hobolt 2006, 641; Vreese 2006). Secondly, they have a strong influence over their constituents and supporters and the capacity to mobilize them in support of one of the voting choices. For these reasons, political elites have such a strong influence on voter behavior that political party support is often the best predictor of a referendum outcome, meaning that voting behaviors are strongly aligned with voters' political allegiances (Baun et al. 2006, 275; Hobolt 2006, 641; Lubbers 2008, 81).

When we turn from referendums in general to peace referendums specifically, such as the Good Friday Agreement in Northern Ireland and the Annan Plan in Cyprus, we see similar instances of influential political leaders and parties (Lordos 2008; Somerville and Kirby 2012). Several factors may contribute to this ability to shape opinion in a peace referendum. First, conflict settings are characterized by highly marked group divisions, especially when ethnicity is a factor. Political parties typically mirror those divisions and voters tend to align with one of them (Horowitz 1985, 298). Second, as peace negotiations are traditionally the prerogative of political elites, political leaders might be a crucial source of information for the media and the wider public; how they frame the agreement is likely to affect the outcome of the vote.

Referendum Campaigns

Referendum campaigners employ a variety of tools to persuade, influence, or simply inform voters. The publication and distribution of informational booklets or pamphlets is one example. More organized campaigns hold public gatherings, meetings, or rallies, and make use of traditional media (television, radio, and newspapers), with internet and social media becoming increasingly important to today's voters. Referendum campaigns have the ability to influence how voters interpret the referendum question(s) and the voting options by highlighting certain aspects or shifting the focus of the subject (Leduc 2002, 716–19; Vreese 2004). Campaigns are usually in favor of one of the voting choices, but there are some nonpartisan, purely informational campaigns.

Political leaders and parties are often involved and can mobilize significant resources, but they are not necessarily the only actors campaigning. Durham (2009, 192–93), whose focus is referendums on international humanitarian law treaties, finds civil society organizations play a crucial role in informing and mobilizing the community to engage in active debates of the implications of the treaty. This, she argues, fosters ownership of the treaty at the local level, which can be particularly relevant in peace agreement referendums. For example, in Northern Ireland, a civil society-led "yes" campaign, described in more detail later in the book, shaped support for the Good Friday Agreement (Hancock 2011).

Public Information and Uncertainty

Referendums ask voters to form an opinion on a particular issue or group of issues that can potentially affect the rules and conditions under which they live. Their decision-making, in addition to the two previous factors, is affected by the amount and quality of information voters have on the issues at stake in the referendum. In addition to political leaders and campaigns, the various forms of media are also important disseminators of information and campaign messages to the masses and can shape public opinion significantly (Vreese 2006, 631–32; Hänggli and Kriesi 2010).

Importantly, the degree of public information shapes the influence that each of two other factors (leaders and campaigns) has on voting behaviors in a referendum. Franklin's Theory posits that voting in a referendum is a test of the performance and popularity of governments in power and does not necessarily address the issue at hand (Franklin et al. 1994, 1995; Franklin 2002). For example, Schneider and Weitsman (1996, 603–5) find that voters' evaluations of the government's performance, as well as their evaluation of the Maastricht Treaty, impacted the european integration referendum results in Denmark, France, and Ireland. However, they also found that when information about the content of the treaty was limited, median voters tended to make their decisions based on their trust of the government's or the opposition's campaign messages. They say this led to stronger and more competitive referendum campaigns. Critics of the theory argue that it views voters as incapable of formulating their own opinions, and that the salience of the issue in the referendum also has the power to explain why voters follow (or do not follow) a political leader's cue (Svensson 2002). In any case, when voters feel they are poorly informed, they tend to look for voting cues from their political leaders, other opinion-makers, or ideologies (Leduc 2002; Hobolt 2006). Therefore, the degree to which political elite preferences affect voting behaviors varies, depending on how informed voters are on the issues.

In cases where the public is not well informed, campaigns have an especially important impact on voter decisions. Leduc (2002, 727) finds that the less informed voters are about the issues prior to the referendum, the more they rely on the campaign period for information and, hence, the more they are influenced by a campaign. Consequently, because voters will tend make their decisions on how to vote closer to the referendum date, the outcome of the referendum will become more unpredictable. Paradigmatically, in the first referendum on the Treaty of Nice in Ireland, the "no" campaign capitalized on voters' lack of information with their "if you don't know, vote no" campaign slogan, tilting support toward the "no" side (Gilland 2002, 532). In peace agreement referendums, campaigns may capitalize on voters' uncertainty (or even fear) about what will happen postreferendum. A good example is the rejection of the Indigenous Rights Accord in Guatemala in 1999, where Lee and Mac Ginty (2012, 54) argue there was a lack of information and time for public debate during the referendum campaigns.

The outcome of a referendum, therefore, is shaped by the dynamics of three interconnected factors: voter knowledge/uncertainty about the issues, political parties' positions, and the nature and strength of referendum campaigns. When voters are less informed on the issues, they will look to their political leaders and the referendum campaigns for information and cues on how to vote. Concomitantly, when voters are less informed, their voting behavior will be more volatile and unpredictable, and they will leave their decision on how to vote to later in the campaign period (Leduc 2002, 727). This augments the influence of a political party's position on voting behaviors and increases the potential influence of referendum campaign messages. If voters are better informed, they will rely less on political leaders' cues and campaign messages.

Agreement Referendum Results as Negotiation Outcomes

Existing studies on peace referendums typically analyze the referendum campaign periods but do not ask how the campaign experience is affected by the conditions of the negotiation process (Rynhold and Cohen 2003; Johansson 2009; Lee and Mac Ginty 2012; Loizides 2014, 2015). Some quantitative studies based on public opinion polls test if certain provisions of a peace agreement have influenced voting behaviors in specific referendums (Rynhold and Cohen 2003; Lordos 2008, 2009; Somerville and Kirby 2012). While explanations drawn from opinion polls can reveal how certain provisions of an agreement shape voting behaviors, they have a limited ability to illuminate the impact of other negotiation and mediation process conditions. Moreover, while authors frequently make recommendations on how referendums can best be used in peacemaking, there is no substantiated body of knowledge on how the peace negotiation process affects these referendums.

The extensive knowledge developed in the wider literature on referendums can be applied fruitfully to the peace negotiation and mediation literature to expand our understanding of peace referendums. From this knowledge of what shapes voting behaviors in referendums, we can now discover if and how peace negotiations shape the outcome of a referendum on a peace agreement; from there, we can begin to understand how the two peacemaking tools can work together.

2

How Peace Negotiations Shape Agreement Referendums

Negotiation Process Conditions

The body of literature on how negotiations are influenced by "audiences" or "constituencies" is so extensive that the examples cited here can only be anecdotal (Iklé 1964; Rubin and Brown 1975; Fearon 1994). For example, with his two-level game theory, Robert Putnam made a major and lasting contribution to scholarship by explaining how political leaders' negotiating behaviors are affected by public expectations or "domestic constraints" (Putnam 1988, 454). One of the factors he explored was how the prospect of having an agreement ratified by a public vote strengthens or weakens political leaders' negotiating positions. I propose that we look at this causal relationship from a new angle. We need to consider the possibility of inverse causality, not looking at how the audience affects the negotiator but the other way around.

Some authors have suggested ways the negotiations may influence referendum outcomes. For example, McGarry and O'Leary (2009, 15–85) contend that the Good Friday Agreement's design, most notably its ability to accommodate the interests of the main political parties, the UUP and Sinn Féin in particular, ensured the success of the referendum in Northern Ireland. Put otherwise, they suggest that the design of an agreement essentially affects its acceptance by voters. However, while the content of an agreement can be crucial to whether political leaders and parties support it in the referendum, as referenced in the previous chapter, political support is only one of the factors that influence voting behaviors in referendums. Therefore, although agreement design might explain why the political parties support an agreement in a referendum, and why the political parties in Northern Ireland did so, it does not necessarily explain why voters supported it.

A second suggestion comes from a study of the failed Guatemalan referendum by Lee and Mac Ginty (2012, 59–60). The authors argue that negotiations with referendums attached to them require broader consultation mechanisms with the people in the communities in conflict. I take up their suggestion in this book and consider whether civil society inclusion in the negotiations affected the Annan Plan and Good Friday Agreement referendums.

Nevertheless, there are other aspects of the negotiations that can potentially influence referendum outcomes, which have not been considered before. Knowing now that referendum results are influenced by the information available to the public on the referendum, by political leaders' and parties' voting preferences, and by the strength and shape of referendum campaigns, other aspects of the negotiations can be thought to affect an agreement referendum result. For example, secretive negotiations can reduce the information available to the public on the issues under negotiation, which could increase voter uncertainty. In addition, whether certain political leaders and/or parties negotiated the agreement or not can expectedly influence their decisions on whether or not to support publicly the agreement in the referendum. Concomitantly, it can influence their decisions on whether, and to what extent, to invest their resources on a referendum campaign. Therefore, exactly who takes part in the negotiations may influence the referendum outcome by shaping political support and determining the organization and strength of the "yes" and "no" campaigns.

Altogether, I hypothesize that four characteristics of peace negotiations can potentially shape the referendum results: the strategies applied by mediators in facilitating an agreement between the parties, the inclusion/exclusion of political actors in/from the negotiations, the same inclusion/exclusion of civil society actors, and the design, or content, of the agreement. I now explore the potential impact of each of these conditions.

Mediation Strategies

There are three types of mediation strategies. Depending on whether the mediator takes a more intrusive or passive role, they fall under three general categories: directive (or *manipulative*), procedural, and communication facilitation. A question central to the study of mediation is which type of mediation strategies and overall mediation styles are more effective in ensuring the success of peace negotiations. In earlier studies on mediation strategy *effectiveness*, the use of directive mediation strategies—the most powerful form of mediator behavior, whereby mediators offer incentives and/or issue ultimatums to push the parties into agreement—was found to be more effective in bringing about partial and full settlements—the latter meaning peace agreements (Bercovitch 1986; Bercovitch and Houston 1993, 2000). This finding supports Touval and Zartman's (1985, 11–13) claim that the ability to pressure the negotiating parties into making concessions, and even committing to a final agreement, is a crucial mediator asset. They, therefore, understood mediation to be a resource-intensive activity most effectively practiced by resourceful actors, such as powerful states, even if biased mediators (Kydd 2003). Henry Kissinger's leveraging of the Israeli and Egyptian governments between 1973 and 1976, by threatening Israel with the withdrawal of military support and enticing Egyptian cooperation by offering closer military and economic ties with the United States, is frequently cited as proof of the greater effectiveness of powerful directive mediation (Sheehan 1976; Rubin 1981; Stein 1985; Mandell and Tomlin 1991).

The same studies on mediation effectiveness found communication facilitation strategies—the most passive type—to be the least effective, yet the most frequently used. This result is unsurprising because facilitating communication—promoting the exchange of information, contact, and cooperation between the parties—is an essential part of any mediator's role and, therefore, is used in every mediation process. Procedural strategies, where mediators exert more control over the formalities of the process, such as determining the agenda, time, and place of the meetings, were found similarly ineffective, or irrelevant to the sorts of outcomes that these studies were interested in (Bercovitch and Houston 2000, 175–76).

With the proliferation of intrastate conflicts in the 1990s, the United Nations emerged as a crucial international mediator. Research on international and regional organizations' mediation efforts found that more passive communication facilitation strategies practiced by their mediators fostered a greater trust in the mediation process (Maoz and Terris 2006). This type of strategy was also found to be more effective in "softening up" (Greig and Diehl 2006) adversarial relationships between the parties and in reducing conflict tension in the long run (Beardsley 2006; Frazier and Dixon 2006). Therefore, even if states were found to be more effective in bringing about the tangible and quantifiable outcomes that earlier studies focused on, international organizations were proven to be more effective conflict managers. It was uncovered then that, while directive mediation strategies are more effective in bringing about agreements, communication facilitation strategies are more effective in improving the relationship between the parties. These findings brought about an extensive debate on the advantages and shortcomings of *pure* vs. *power* mediation and the associated debates on the limits of mediation and mediator impartiality. This led to growing consensus in the field that the strategies are complementary and, as the proponents of multiparty mediation suggest (Crocker, Hampson, and Aall 1999), the key to mediation success is their adequate or timely combination (Bercovitch and Gartner 2009; Carment, Yiagadeesen, and Achkar 2009; Quinn et al. 2006).

Since then, other types of medium- to long-term outcomes have been considered in the study of what type of mediation strategies are more effective. Once it was taken into account that a mediation process can hardly be deemed successful if the agreement reached is not implemented, the durability of the agreement became a new outcome of study. Svensson (2007, 244) found that while power mediators are more effective at brokering peace agreements, mediators using less intrusive, *pure* mediation styles are more likely to bring about agreements that are ultimately implemented. Peace agreements reached under pure mediation tend to include provisions, such as sharing territory or political power, that feature in more durable agreements. Beardsley et al. (2006) proposed a differentiated approach to the study of success or effectiveness in international crises. They quantitatively analyze what types of mediation strategies are more effective in bringing about three different types of outcomes: "formal agreement," "tension reduction," and "crisis abatement." They find each outcome is related to a different mediation strategy and suggest that the contradictory results in the study of the effectiveness of mediation strategies could be explained by how individual researchers have considered the outcome variable. Beardsley (2011) has since stressed that a more comprehensive approach to mediation outcomes, sensitive to both the short and long term, is needed to truly evaluate not only the effectiveness, but also the overall impact of mediation on conflict resolution.

The study of the effectiveness of mediation strategies and the associated discussion of what mediation "success" is has, therefore, greatly evolved throughout the past couple of decades. I propose studying yet another outcome, an agreement referendum result as a mediation outcome. I, therefore, pose the question of whether mediator behaviors can ultimately shape agreement referendums. If so, and since scholars have found again and again that the effectiveness of mediation strategies varies depending on the outcome that is considered, I ask what types of mediation strategies are more effective if we consider whether the peace agreement was accepted in the referendum or not as the mediation outcome.

There are a few possibilities here. Beginning with directive strategies, the use of leverage—either through pressure or an incentive—to push the parties into an agreement can potentially affect whether and how political leaders support it in the referendum. Leveraging is associated with agreement implementation problems, primarily due to creating an "artificial" enticement or motivation for the parties to reach an agreement. That enticement or pressure then dissipates once the agreement is signed and the mediator exits the conflict. For the same reason, political leaders who are pressured into agreement will potentially be less willing to support and campaign for an agreement in a referendum. Furthermore, political leaders or parties who have been pressured or enticed into an agreement may only maintain support for it in the referendum if the pressure or enticement remains in place.

Another mediation tactic that can shape referendum outcomes is the degree of secrecy surrounding negotiations. Reducing the visibility of a negotiation process may help participants talk more openly, cooperate more easily, and save face, especially if they are making unpopular concessions. Although secrecy is an important feature of peace negotiations, it has not yet been widely discussed, possibly because it is seen as indispensable and unavoidable. However, recent studies of the Oslo Accords between the Israeli government and the Palestine Liberation Organization have begun to consider the negative impact of secrecy on peace processes. To decrease the visibility of the talks, the Oslo negotiations were held in Norway and the two delegations were composed of individuals other than the leaders: lower-ranking members of the Palestinian Liberation Organization represented the PLO, and a team of academics represented the Israeli government. While secrecy promoted cooperation and agreement, it diminished the incentive and the capacity for political leaders to foster support for the agreement at home, especially for the Israeli government (Pruitt 1997, 246; Kriesberg 2001; Wanis-St. John 2011). This effect can be especially problematic if a referendum is held following the negotiations. By reducing political leaders' ability to "sell" the agreement, secrecy can reduce political support for a peace agreement. Further, political leaders may feel it is too risky to publicly support and campaign for an agreement that their constituents know little about and, for that reason, may be skeptical of and be less likely to endorse it in a referendum.

This leads directly into another problem resulting from secrecy. The secrecy surrounding a negotiation process may influence the amount or accuracy of the information available to the public on the issues being negotiated. The availability of information or its lack may also dictate the start and/or the depth of public debate. Durham (2009, 192–93) argues that support for a treaty or agreement is fostered by informing and educating communities, creating a genuine discussion between ordinary people on the implications of ratifying it. Similarly, Lee and Mac Ginty (2012, 59) stress the need for sufficient time for public discussion and education before a referendum. By reducing information availability, secrecy may reduce support for the agreement in the referendum, potentially by contributing to greater public uncertainty about the benefits and disadvantages of the agreement and preventing timely public debate.

Spoiler Management/Political Inclusion

Whether a political leader or party is included in the negotiations may determine whether, or how well, an agreement addresses that leader's or party's interests. Whose interests should be accommodated and which actors should or should not be included in peace negotiations is a topic of ongoing debate in the literature. Over twenty years ago, Stedman (1997; 2002) advised mediators to exclude from peace negotiations those leaders who benefit from the status quo and have incentives to oppose a peace process. Such leaders, or *spoilers*, perceive a peace process as threatening to their power, worldview, or interests, and may use violence or other means to undermine it. Stedman (1997, 9–11) argued that some types of spoilers can be included in the negotiations, while others should be at arm's length. Spoilers with limited or flexible ("greedy") goals can potentially be accommodated and should be included in the negotiations. "Total" spoilers, on the other hand, are committed only to their own hegemonic goals and are unwilling to accommodate others; hence, they should be excluded.

"Spoiling" may negatively impact a peace process by causing delays or forcing the postponement or cancelation of talks; it may even prevent the implementation of an agreement after it is reached. Zahar (2003, 118–22) warns against the danger of peace negotiations actually creating spoilers by profiling actors as such. These actors, she argues, may attempt to undermine peace negotiations not necessarily to derail the peace negotiations but to signal their desire to be at the negotiating table or to express concerns over the agreement's implementation (Zahar 2003, 270). "Spoiling" may actually result in the introduction of new issues into the negotiations, give marginalized groups a voice, or bring new actors into the talks (Newman and Richmond 2006, 109). Zahar contests Stedman's typology on the grounds that profiling an actor as a spoiler is risky and ignores the possibility that the attitudes and positions of certain actors or groups are not fixed and may change over time. To her, inclusiveness is crucial to avoid giving anyone an incentive to renege during settlement implementation.

This is especially relevant for peace agreement referendums. Excluding certain actors from the process leading to the referendum can create incentives for them to campaign against the agreement, while greater political inclusion may elicit support. Those who negotiate an agreement are naturally more likely to be invested in its approval and implementation. Put otherwise, which political representatives are included in a negotiation process may shape political support for a peace agreement and the relative strength of the campaigns leading up to a referendum, thereby influencing the results.

Civil Society Inclusion

Civil society can serve a peace process in multiple ways. Civil society inclusion has had a legitimizing effect on mediation processes and their resulting agreements in many cases, including Kenya (Zanker 2013), Congo, and Northern Ireland (Rao 2010). It has helped to foster peace negotiations in Sierra Leone (Aljets, Chacko, and Jessop 2008) and Liberia (Zanker 2013). The mediation of the Economic Community of West African States (ECOWAS) in Liberia is particularly interesting; representatives of civil society groups were invited to take part in the negotiations and were encouraged to pressure the parties to settle[1] (Zanker 2013). Civil society groups have also led successful peace mediation processes in Mozambique[2] and Tunisia[3].

In addition to promoting peace agreements that are balanced and more widely perceived as legitimate, the inclusion of civil society during peace negotiations favors the implementation of an agreement and the durability of peace (Nilsson 2012). Civil society groups are in close contact with the public and can function as communication channels between the negotiations and the wider communities (Paffenholz, Kew, and Wanis-St. John 2006, 68–70). Including civil society in peace negotiations can also guarantee that the interests of the wider society are considered, not just the interests of the elite. This can generate both greater elite accountability and grassroots ownership of an agreement and ensure that key constituencies and stakeholder interests are included.

The activities of civil society groups, therefore, are increasingly understood as aiding peace processes, from ripening

1. Representatives of the Mano River Women's Peace Network, the Inter-Religious Council on Liberia, the Liberian Bar Association, and members of the Liberian Diaspora were invited by the mediator to participate in the negotiations between the Charles Taylor government, Liberians United for Reconciliation and Democracy (LURD), and the Movement for Democracy in Liberia (MODEL) in 2003 (Zanker 2013).

2. The Community of Sant'Egidio, a lay organization of Catholics, mediated the Rome General Peace Accords of 1992 between the Mozambique Liberation Front (FRELIMO) government and the rebel Mozambican National Resistance; this marked the end of almost two decades of civil war.

3. The Tunisian National Dialogue Quartet, an alliance of the Tunisian General Labour Union (UGTT), the Tunisian Confederation of Industry, Trade and Handicrafts (UTICA), the Tunisian Human Rights League (LTDH), and the Tunisian Order of Lawyers, mediated political party talks on Tunisia's democratic transition, 2013–14.

negotiations to favoring implementation. The role of civil society in peace process referendums is less well understood. Civil society groups have the potential to be important referendum campaigners (Durham 2009; Hancock 2011); however, the degree to which they are involved with the negotiation process may shape how active and mobilized they are during the referendum. As civil society inclusion is known to aid peace processes, we should expect that its inclusion in peace negotiations favors the "yes" campaign and a wider dissemination of public information, positively impacting support for the peace agreement in a referendum.

Agreement Design

Peace agreement referendums typically ask voters if they accept or support the implementation of the agreement reached. Since the onus of the referendum is on the agreement, the content of these documents can be expected to have a considerable impact on referendum results. As already mentioned, the content of a peace agreement can be influential in determining the political support that it receives in a referendum. Some have argued that specific provisions in these agreements are crucial to gathering political support. Supporters of consociationalism, for example, draw on the Northern Ireland case to argue that the only realistic way to achieve a stable solution to conflict in divided societies is to set up power-sharing institutions (O'Leary and McGarry 1993; McGarry and O'Leary 2006a, 2009). To them, power-sharing agreements are the key to accommodating groups with competing interests. Haass (1991) and Stedman (1991) highlight that other factors are at play here. The ability of political leaders to commit to an agreement is influenced by their capacity to convince their political allies and constituents that the agreement is to their benefit. The arrival at an agreement also depends on how well its "formula" is able to solve leaders' problems in publicly committing to an agreement with former enemies.

Considering both, we can expect that in peace negotiations with agreement referendums, the extent to which the provisions of an agreement satisfy the interests of the political leaders who have negotiated it, and/or their ability to "sell" it to their constituencies, will sway their decision to support it in the referendum. It can also determine whether or not they will campaign in the referendum and, if so, for or against it. Therefore, agreement design can potentially affect the shape and strength of the "yes" and "no" campaigns by shaping political leaders' and parties' decisions to campaign for or against it and with what resources. We can then expect that, when an agreement accommodates differing political interests, it is likely to receive greater political support and strengthen the "yes" campaign and, thereby potentially increase support for the agreement in the referendum.

However, the content of an agreement can also more directly shape voters' decision-making in referendums, depending on how well informed they are about its content. We must therefore consider that the extent to which voters are informed about the agreement will moderate how influenced they are by political leaderships and campaign messages.

Contextual and Other Factors

Peace referendum results are influenced by factors unrelated to the peace negotiation process. Before exploring whether and how all of the above negotiation process factors have an impact on referendum outcomes, it is important to note that referendum experiences and results are not only influenced by them. Referendum results are greatly shaped by the context in which they take place. In peace referendums many of these factors have to do with the specific challenges that holding a referendum in conflict settings poses. Other determining factors derive more generally from the rules and procedures of holding a referendum.

Starting with the influence of the context, Lee and Mac Ginty (2012, 50–58) say three "contextual" factors have led to peace referendum "failures" around the world. The first is a lack of broad consultation of important constituencies during negotiations, particularly in Guatemala (1999), Iraq (2005), or Cyprus (2004), and the second is a lack of voter education, which they attribute to the minimal time for public debate that peace referendum campaign periods traditionally offer. However, I understand the first issue to be a condition of the negotiation process, not a contextual factor, and I treat it and study it in this book as a question of inclusion. As for the second, although voter education can be understood as a contextual condition, I explore whether it is affected by negotiation process conditions. Insecurity is the third factor mentioned by the authors. As they point out, in the referendums in Guatemala, Iraq, and Rwanda (2003), insecurity, mistrust, and fear of postreferendum instability strongly affected the results, whether instigating rejectionism (Guatemala) or motivating support (Rwanda). Fears related to the survival of a culture can also shape referendum results. Lubbers (2008, 80–83) found that the Dutch "no" to the European Constitution in 2005 was impacted by a perception of EU integration as a threat to the survival of Dutch culture, particularly among less educated voters. Such fears can be particularly salient in peace referendums and exacerbated by insecurity.

Contextual conditions are crucial to the experience and outcome of referendums in peace processes; most scholars who study them agree that to avoid their negative consequences and potential failures, the context of the referendum must be carefully considered and prepared (Lee and Mac Ginty 2012; Loizides 2015, 134; Collin 2018). For this reason, Loizides

(2014) asserts that the *timing* of a peace referendum can be decisive and is particularly important for peace agreement referendums and their need for a specific outcome: a "yes" vote.

Socioeconomic conditions also have an effect on voter decisions, especially in treaty or agreement referendums whose implementation is likely to bring social and economic changes. For example, in Poland, fears about the impact of EU membership on agriculture, state-owned heavy industry, small- and medium-sized businesses, and banking economic sectors mobilized rejectionists and reduced public support for EU integration prior to Polish accession in 2004 (Szczerbiak 2001, 114–15). Similarly, Sciarini and Listhaug (1997, 431–33) argue that the Swiss rejection of European Union membership in 1994 and the Norwegian rejection of the European Economic Area in 1992 happened because EU membership was not seen as an economic necessity by voters. Consequently, concerns about the defense of traditions and national sovereignty became especially pronounced during the referendum campaign period. In Cyprus, for example, EU accession has been seen as a determining factor in the Annan Plan referendum, in both the Greek Cypriot "no" vote and the Turkish Cypriot "yes" (Bahcheli 2004; Lordos 2008).

Lastly, referendum results naturally depend on who is asked or allowed to vote in the referendum and, of course, on who actually turns out to vote on the day of the referendum. Voter turnout in peace referendums markedly differs from case to case. For example, the referendums in South Sudan and Rwanda had extremely high turnout rates, above 90 percent, but the one in Guatemala had an extremely low turnout rate of 19 percent. Colombia was higher, at 37 percent, but was still disappointing. Low referendum turnouts are problematic; they raise questions about how representative the results are and the legitimacy of implementing the outcome of the referendum.

Although some of the factors mentioned here are unavoidably connected to decisions made within the negotiating process, they are not themselves a characteristic of the peace negotiations and, therefore, are not included in my hypotheses. For example, as mentioned in the previous chapter, who is eligible to vote in a referendum can be a highly problematic issue in peace negotiations, but it is not affected by the proceedings of the negotiations per se. Nonetheless, all the contextual and other factors enumerated here may influence a referendum result and need to be taken into account in any analysis of the conditions that shape peace referendums.

3

The Case Studies

The Cyprus and Northern Ireland Conflicts

The conflicts in Cyprus and Northern Ireland have some surprising and significant similarities. To begin with, both regions have a history of British colonialism, and their respective conflicts erupted during the decolonization process. In Cyprus, as the British were signaling their departure in the 1950s, Greek Cypriots began fighting for *enosis*, or unification with "motherland" Greece (Anderson 2008, 2). Fearing Greek Cypriot domination, Turkish Cypriots reacted with anti-union demonstrations expressing a desire for *taksim*, or the division of the island between Greece and Turkey (Yilmaz and Ercan 2005, 30). As the struggle threatened to evolve into a regional war, in 1959, the United Kingdom brokered an agreement with Greece and Turkey that led to the foundation of the Republic of Cyprus in 1960.

The power-sharing arrangement collapsed a short three years later. Friction between Greek Cypriot and Turkish Cypriot leaders over the interpretation of the constitutional provisions gave rise to a period of ongoing constitutional crisis, government paralysis, and increasing communal tensions (Anderson 2008, 8). Communal clashes and the impending threat of Turkish military involvement pushed the United Nations to intervene. The UN Peacekeeping Force in Cyprus

(UNFICYP) was deployed in 1964, and the secretary-general mandated to lead the peacemaking mission.

An uneasy peace prevailed until a military junta overthrew the Papandreou government in Greece. A split between Athens and the Greek Cypriot leadership began to emerge as the Greek Cypriot President Makarios became wary of unifying Cyprus with the dictatorship (Solsten 1993). This marked a definitive turn in Greek Cypriot aspirations, from the pursuit of *enosis* to the pursuit of an independent Greek Cypriot–led republic, where the Turkish Cypriot community would be granted minority status.

In July 1974, the Greek junta attempted to take over the island, prompting Turkey to military action. To separate the opposing forces, UNFICYP established ceasefire lines and a buffer zone across the island. The territory north of the UN buffer zone came under control of the Turkish army. In 1983, the Turkish Republic of Northern Cyprus (TRNC) was unilaterally proclaimed, although it is not internationally recognized by any state, except Turkey. South of the Green Line, the Republic of Cyprus continued to be administrated by Greek Cypriots. Throughout the years, continuous mediation initiatives launched by UN secretaries-general were repeatedly able to bring Greek Cypriot and Turkish Cypriot political leaders to the negotiation table, but no peace agreement ever materialized.

The conflict in Northern Ireland has some similar root causes, and the divisions between the communities there emerged under similar circumstances. When Ireland became a Free State in 1922, the northern Ulster provinces remained part of the United Kingdom of Great Britain and Northern Ireland. The borders of the new state of Northern Ireland were drawn to encompass the Protestant majority, who wished to remain part of the United Kingdom—the *Unionist* community. This majority remained fearful of Irish nationalist aspirations, seeing these as a threat to their religious and British cultural traditions, and to their political and territorial union with Great Britain (Hennessey 1997, 3). Meanwhile, the *Nationalist*, mainly Catholic, minority community felt cut off from their Irish identity and trapped in a Unionist-dominated political establishment that discriminated against them and excluded them from power (McKittrick and McVea 2002, 5–6). In 1968, a civil rights march in Derry erupted into violence and rioting after confrontations between Catholic protesters and the Royal Ulster Constabulary (RUC)—the mainly Protestant Northern Ireland police force (Lee 1990, 420–21). In August 1969, with the "troubles" spreading from Derry to Belfast and across Northern Ireland, British troops were deployed to contain the escalating violence.

The Republic of Ireland was initially reluctant to get involved. The members of Sinn Féin, its largest political party, disagreed on whether Irish unity should be pursued. The divisions translated into a split in the Irish Republican Army (IRA), which had fought for Irish independence from Britain. Dissident members formed the Provisional IRA (PIRA) and declared war against what they saw as the British occupation of the north (Bew 2007, 450). The PIRA—the *republican* paramilitaries—pledged to fight for the unity of the Irish Republic. In parallel, in the Unionist camp, the *loyalist* paramilitaries (because of their professed loyalty to the British Crown) returned to activity in the 1960s to defend the Protestant community (Fitzduff 2002, 8–9). The Ulster Volunteer Force (UVF) and the Ulster Defence Association/Ulster Freedom Fighters (UDA/UFF) were the most significant of these groups.

The activities of the Republican and Loyalist paramilitaries shaped the ensuing conflict; together, they were responsible for 90 percent of the deaths, bombings, shootings, kidnappings, intimidation, and terror in Northern Ireland (Fitzduff

2002, 8–9). The barricades put up by the paramilitaries eventually became permanent brick "peacelines" drawing a territorial and physical separation between the two communities (McKittrick and McVea 2002, 55–56).

In March 1972, the Parliament collapsed when the largest nationalist political party at the time, the Social Democratic and Labour Party (SDLP), abandoned it, and direct rule from Westminster was established. The collapse of the Northern Irish political institutions, coupled with the realization that it could not militarily defeat the PIRA, led Britain to search for a solution to the conflict that would entail a deep transformation of the political establishment in Northern Ireland (McGrattan 2010, 59–60).

As the above synopsis makes clear, the two conflicts have more in common than their colonial roots. Both conflicts engaged communities that were divided along ethnic lines and asymmetrical in size: the Irish Unionist and Greek Cypriot communities are majoritarian, while the Irish Nationalist and Turkish Cypriot communities are minorities. Both are longstanding and intractable conflicts, with physical boundaries increasing segregation. In both cases, an important factor in intractability has been the involvement of external actors. The Nationalist and Unionist communities regard Ireland and Britain, respectively, as supporters of their mutually exclusive interests in the face of a threatening "other" community. Similarly, Greek Cypriots and Turkish Cypriots regard Greece and Turkey, respectively, as protectors and supporters of their cause.

The Peace Processes

The growth of the European Community (EC), later the European Union (EU), served, in both Cyprus and Northern Ireland, to hasten the start of the peace negotiations that eventually produced the Annan Plan and the Good Friday

Agreement. The period that preceded the Annan Plan negotiations was marked by rising tensions and military build-up on the island after Greek Cypriot President George Vassiliou submitted Cyprus's application to the EU in 1992. Turkish and Turkish Cypriot leaders strongly protested this action; they claimed the Greek Cypriot government had no right to act on behalf of the entire island. EU membership became a pivotal issue in the Cypriot peace negotiations especially when United States Special Envoy Richard Holbrooke—who mediated the Dayton Agreements ending the war in the Balkans in 1995—advocated for a negotiated solution to be made a precondition to Cypriot EU accession[1] (Michael 2011, 148–49).

Holbrooke's mediation strategy set the groundwork for the Annan Plan process. The negotiations that produced the Annan Plan were launched by UN Secretary-General Kofi Annan in 1999 in an effort to reach a peace settlement that would allow Cyprus to join the EU as a united country. From 1999 to March 2004, Annan's special representative to Cyprus, Álvaro de Soto, mediated the negotiations between the Greek Cypriot and Turkish Cypriot leaders. As agreed between the leaders, the final text of the agreement did not require their endorsement. Rather, it was left to each of the communities to refuse or accept it in separate but simultaneous referendums in both the north and the south of the divided island.

The United Kingdom and Ireland's accession to the EU (the Economic Community, at the time) in 1972 compelled Britain and Ireland to work together on a solution to the

1. After the end of the Cold War, Cyprus remained of strategic interest to the US. The Cyprus conflict weakened NATO and limited EU expansion. Turkey was perceived as crucial to American interests in the unstable Middle East and a vital ally in close geographic proximity to Iran, Syria, and Iraq, and the British military bases in Cyprus were of strategic importance for the US in the Gulf crisis (Savvides 1998, 49–50).

Northern Ireland conflict (Byrne, 2000, 3, 17). In March 1973, the British proposed the establishment of a power-sharing arrangement to replace the majority rule of the Northern Irish parliament. The resulting Sunningdale Agreement created a new power-sharing government but, just as in Cyprus, it was short-lived. Protestant fears that the Council represented a first step toward Irish unity and the resulting lack of support from an increasingly divided Unionist community caused Sunningdale's collapse a few months later (Barton 2009, 16–17).

The British government continued to look for a power-sharing solution in the following two decades. In the Anglo-Irish Agreement of 1985, Britain granted Ireland a consultative role in Northern Ireland affairs. Later, in the Downing Street Declaration of 1993, it declared its respect for Irish unity if that were the wish of the majority of the people of Northern Ireland. The agreements, together with the Clinton administration's efforts to persuade Sinn Féin to pursue its goals politically, were instrumental in getting the paramilitaries to agree to a cease-fire, thus allowing the peace negotiations leading to the Good Friday Agreement to begin.

Both the Good Friday Agreement and the Annan Plan offered democratic solutions and both provided for power-sharing consociational forms of government. Both negotiation processes faced stalemates over issues and time-consuming navigation of procedural matters, evasions, and media leaks; keeping the negotiations alive became an important goal for the mediators and their teams (Mitchell 1999; United Nations 2003). The reasons for this differed. Former US Senator George Mitchell, who mediated the negotiations in Northern Ireland, needed the negotiation process to survive and succeed to avoid the re-escalation of paramilitary violence, while Álvaro de Soto needed to seize what was perceived as a historically auspicious moment for agreement, given Cyprus' EU candidacy.

The separate and simultaneous referendums on the ratification of the Annan Plan were held on April 24, 2004. A simultaneous majority "yes" vote was required from both communities for the agreement to be accepted. It was rejected by 66 percent of the people across Cyprus, but the majority of the voters in the Turkish Cypriot community supported it (United Nations 2004, para. 72). Similarly, two referendums were held simultaneously for the GFA to be ratified. As per the terms of the agreement, Republic of Ireland's constitutional claim to Northern Ireland had to be amended, which required a referendum. The majority of the people in Northern Ireland voted in favor of the agreement on May 22, 1998, and the constitutional change was also—overwhelmingly—accepted in the Republic of Ireland.

Explanations of the Annan Plan and Good Friday Agreement Outcomes

A handful of studies have compared specific aspects of the Cypriot and Northern Irish peace processes. Some focus on the role of external parties in the conflict mediation (Byrne 2000; Kocadal 2016). Others consider how the EU affected the process (Tannam 2012), and still others look at political parties' ethnic outbidding during the peace process (Moore et al. 2013). The two peace negotiations have not yet been consistently compared; more importantly, neither have the two referendums. Notably, all four process conditions proposed in this book—mediation strategies, political inclusion, civil society inclusion, and agreement design—are part of existing explanations of the "failed" Annan Plan referendum or the "successful" Good Friday Agreement referendum, or both.

Mediation strategies are significant in both cases. Several scholars say the UN's mediation strategies were responsible for the failure of the Annan Plan. Their arguments center on two factors: secrecy and arbitration. The secrecy of the Annan Plan negotiations is said to have contributed to the rejection of the agreement because it prevented the process from involving and gaining the support of social groups beyond the political elites (Drath 2004; Michael 2007; Lordos 2009). The use of arbitration—under which the secretary-general decided on the issues that were not agreed upon at the last round of negotiations—is said to have removed the political leaders' accountability for the final agreement and allowed them to campaign against it (Kaymak 2012, 106). Some also say the UN overpressured the leaders by using the EU accession date as a deadline for agreement (Drath 2004, 349). In contrast, George Mitchell's mediation is said to have contributed to the success of the GFA. The three-strand negotiation process design and the decoupling of the decommissioning issue from the main negotiations are two procedural strategies considered to have positively impacted the process (Curran and Sebenius 2003, 135–37).

These explanations are limited in two ways, however. First, in the Annan Plan, although Turkish Cypriot leaders were subject to the same mediation strategies as Greek Cypriot leaders, authors use the strategies to explain Greek Cypriot rejection without considering Turkish Cypriot acceptance. Michael (2007, 597–98) is an exception in arguing that the major flaw in the Annan strategy was that UN mediators focused on sidelining Turkish Cypriot leader Rauf Denktash, while naively taking Greek Cypriot support for granted. Second, in both cases, authors generally take "success" to mean the agreement's acceptance in the referendum and "failure" to mean its rejection, while conducting little analysis of the referendum campaign experience itself. Therefore, their assessments of the impact of a mediation strategy may not explain referendum results. In addition, and now comparing explanations in the two cases, although negotiation secrecy is seen as an important factor in the failure of the Annan Plan negotiations, it has not been considered in analyses of the GFA negotiations and mediation.

Spoiler management and political inclusion are also seen as relevant to the outcomes in the two cases. The exclusion (or "sidelining") of certain actors is said to have allowed the agreement to be reached in both processes. By "allowing" the hardliner Democratic Unionist Party (DUP) and United Kingdom Unionist Party (UKUP) parties to leave and continuing the negotiations without them in 1997, George Mitchell is said to have successfully sidelined potential spoilers (Durkan 1999, 36–43). Similarly, in the Annan Plan negotiations, the sidelining of Turkish Cypriot leader Rauf Denktash is considered to have been a necessary means to reaching a final agreement (Michael 2007, 598). The inclusion of Sinn Féin, on the other hand, is seen favorably as a factor in the group's transformation from spoiler to stakeholder, and as fundamental to the implementation of the agreement (Darby 2001, 15–26). In fact, the overall inclusivity of the GFA negotiations, which included the majority of the political parties in Northern Ireland, is said to have helped the parties reach an agreement. Inclusivity, it is argued, strengthened the more moderate positions and political parties (Curran and Sebenius 2003, 150–51) and favored implementation by addressing the interests of different stakeholders (McGarry and O'Leary 2006a, 256–57). While most agree that political inclusion/exclusion favored Northern Irish "success," the impact on the referendum result has not been singled out for study. And while the significance of inclusion has been discussed for Northern Ireland, the fact that the negotiations in Cyprus drew only on the parties in government has not yet been considered.

Scholars studying both cases also see civil society involvement and public engagement as important explanatory factors of each outcome. On the one hand, in Northern Ireland, civil society helped create intercommunal contacts and back-channel communication avenues during the negotiations (Cochrane 2000, 2006; Hancock 2001) and put pressure on political leaders to bring the negotiations to a successful end (Cochrane 2000, 2001, 2006; Bell and O'Rourke 2007). In addition, the civil society–led "yes" campaign in Northern Ireland is considered to have been vital to getting the "yes" vote above the 50 percent threshold in the Unionist community (Hancock 2011). On the other hand, the failure to engage the grassroots and include civil society in the negotiations is said to have contributed to the failure of the Annan Plan in Cyprus (Lordos 2009), arguably because civil society initiatives were not recognized as a valuable policy option at the political level (Hadjipavlou 2002, 15). While the lack of civil society inclusion in the negotiations is seen to have contributed to the Greek Cypriot rejection of the Annan Plan, the impact on the Turkish Cypriot vote has not been discussed. In addition, if civil society played a crucial role in the GFA referendum, we do not know whether the inclusion of civil society actors in the negotiations per se was a contributing factor there.

Finally, explanations for the respective "failure" and "success" of the Annan Plan and the GFA processes have also drawn on the agreements' designs. The "constructive" ambiguity of some of the provisions of the GFA was arguably essential to getting the Nationalist and Unionist parties to sign the agreement (Tonge and Evans 2002; Dixon 2013). In the Cypriot case, on the other hand, it has been suggested that the attempt to "fill in the gaps" led to an agreement that failed to address Greek Cypriot leaders' concerns (Drath 2004). While these arguments suggest the agreements' design determined the ensuing political support for the agreements in the referendum, again, political support is merely one of many factors affecting referendum outcomes. Notwithstanding, exit polls show that Greek Cypriot voters voted against the Annan Plan due to its security provisions—essentially, because it did not provide for the complete withdrawal of Turkish troops from the island (Lordos 2009). However, President Papadopoulos pinpointed this specific provision of the agreement when asking Greek Cypriots to vote "no" in the referendum just days before it was held (PIO 2004a). It is possible, then, that the "no" votes were not directly shaped by the content of the agreement, but by how the security provisions were framed by the president.

Overall, with some exceptions, existing explanations of "success" and "failure" in Northern Ireland and Cyprus tend to consider why an agreement was reached by the political representatives, and not necessarily why it was accepted or rejected in the referendum. The two outcomes are often not differentiated but treated as a single outcome. With a few exceptions (Michael 2007; Kaymak 2012), analyses of how negotiations affected referendums inadvertently assume a perfect political alignment in voter behavior. In other words, there frequently exists an assumption that voters linearly followed the leaders or political parties. Although this might be the case, if they do not acknowledge this assumption, such arguments on the impact of negotiation process conditions will ignore the fact that the referendum campaign period can shape voting behaviors. In not considering the impact that the campaign experience has on referendum voters, such explanations will only actually speak to why the agreement was reached or not, and not why it was rejected or accepted in the referendum.

Case Selection

The selection of the Annan Plan and Good Friday Agreement negotiations and referendums for comparison is due primarily to their opposing referendum outcomes. Choosing two cases where the outcome was the same could lead to confirmation bias and overemphasis on certain characteristics of the process. Beyond the similarities in the historical circumstances leading to the conflicts and the already-mentioned characteristics of the conflict and the parties, the referendums themselves exhibit salient similarities. Being agreement referendums, both asked voters whether or not they supported the implementation of the peace agreement and in both the results were binding—not merely consultative, as some referendums are. Both were also universal plebiscites, with all voters, not just a specific group or community allowed to vote. Adding to the comparability of the referendums, voter turnout in both cases was over 80 percent (Melaugh and McKenna 1998; United Nations 2004, para. 72).

Equally interesting are the comparative outcomes within the respective communities. Although the Annan Plan was rejected because only 24 percent of the Greek Cypriot community supported it, 65 percent of the Turkish Cypriot community voted "yes" (United Nations 2004, para. 72). There was a similar divide in Northern Ireland. Approximately 96–97 percent of the Nationalist community voted "yes" in the referendum, compared to 51–53 percent of the Unionist community (Melaugh and McKenna 1998). Therefore, the difference between the rates of support from each community in the respective referendums is around 40 percent. It should be noted that the Annan Plan formally required a majority "yes" vote from both communities to be ratified, but the Good Friday Agreement did not. In the latter, only a majority of "yes" votes overall was required. Nonetheless, as Rynhold and Cohen (2003, para. 90) argue, it was crucial for the legitimacy of the GFA, and a concern during the referendum campaign period, that a majority in both communities support it (this will be discussed in a later chapter). Therefore, to an extent, the ratification of both agreements required majority support from all concerned communities.

There are, however, some important contextual differences between the two cases, with implications for the referendum experiences and results that need to be considered. While the

Cyprus conflict is a *frozen* conflict, where violence has not taken place since 1975, paramilitary violence was a feature of the Northern Ireland conflict and peace process well beyond the referendum (although there was a change in intensity and type of violence with the start of the negotiation process). The threat of the escalation of violence might have weighed on voters' decision-making in Northern Ireland, but not necessarily in Cyprus. Another vital distinction is that the Greek Cypriot and Turkish Cypriot communities have not lived together since the buffer zone was created in 1975, regaining limited contact after the first crossing point was opened in the buffer zone in 2003. In contrast, the Irish communities have always lived together—with some segregated areas. As a result of greater proximity, the referendum was more of a shared experience in Northern Ireland than in Cyprus.

Research Design

In order to study if and how negotiation process conditions have an impact on referendum results, an entirely new research design is needed—one that is able to explore causal links between the two phenomena. To that end, I put forward in this book a qualitative design that explores whether and how each of the hypothesized negotiation process conditions—*mediation strategies*, *political inclusion*, *civil society inclusion*, and *agreement design*—influenced each of the conditions found to determine referendum outcomes—*political party support*, *referendum campaigns*, and *public information and uncertainty*. Although I study the impact of the negotiation process variables on each of the referendum determinants individually, the referendum outcome is a product of their interplay as well as other factors, as will be shown.

I examine if and how the negotiation process variables had an impact on the overall Annan Plan and GFA referendum results, but also if and how they shaped the communal referendum outcomes. This is especially interesting not only because the differences in the percentages of support between the communities in each case are similar, but also because the results across the four communities are so different:

- Nationalist support for GFA: 96–97 percent
- Turkish Cypriot support for Annan: 65 percent
- Unionist support for GFA: 51–53 percent
- Greek Cypriot support for Annan: 23 percent

Referendum results can create or reinforce perceptions of winners and losers in peace processes. By comparing the communities' support within and across cases, the results will be more sensitive to potential differences in the communities' experience of the negotiations and show whether the negotiations contributed to the polarization of support. In the upcoming chapters I begin by examining each of the two case studies individually and compare the findings on each of the cases later on, drawing comparisons across the four communities as well.

Negotiation Process Variables

Mediation strategies. One of the goals set out in this study is to explore if and what kind of mediator strategies potentially influence support in an agreement referendum. This variable is understood in broad terms and to encompass all types of mediator behaviors, not just the three types of mediation strategies mentioned earlier. One aspect is the arbitration, or meditration, procedure used in the Annan Plan negotiations; this has not been categorized as a type of mediation strategy because scholars do not agree whether the use of arbitration practices in Cyprus (and also in Kosovo) goes beyond the boundaries of a mediator's role (see, for example, Ross and Conlon 2000; Belloni 2009; Ker-Lindsay 2009).

Communication and coordination with external parties with close relationships to local communities is fundamental to the progress and success of a mediation initiative and is therefore a crucial mediator task. For this reason, I also examine how mediators involve "kin-states"[2] in negotiations as mediation strategy. The degree to which Greece and Turkey were involved in the Annan Plan negotiations differed substantially from that of Britain and Ireland in the GFA negotiations. Britain and Ireland were pragmatic about working together to expedite an agreement during Mitchell's mediation and, for this reason, have been described as "quasi-mediators" (Byrne 2000). Therefore, in my analysis of the impact of mediation strategies, I look at their influence.

It must be noted that in both the Annan Plan and Good Friday Agreement negotiations the roles played by Álvaro de Soto (Cyprus) and George Mitchell (Northern Ireland) are not officially referred to as "mediation." In Cyprus, Álvaro de Soto provided the "good offices" of the secretary-general, while George Mitchell "chaired" the All-Party Talks. Nonetheless, they both played mediating roles; as in the literature (for example, Richmond 1998; Curran and Sebenius 2003; Curran, Sebenius, and Watkins 2004; Michael 2007), they are referred to and analyzed in this book as mediators.

Political inclusion. Another aim is to ascertain whether differences in the participation of political stakeholders had an impact on the referendum outcomes. Political inclusion refers to if and how different parties across the political spectrum were included in the negotiation process. There are many ways a political leader, party, or actor can be included in peace negotiations. Beyond formal participation, a political party or political leader can participate indirectly, for example, in formal or

2. Kocadal (2016) defines "kin-states" as "those states whose dominant ethnic group identifies with a co-ethnic population that transcends the borders of that state" (172).

informal consultations with mediators. For this reason, I prefer the term "inclusion" to "representation," as political representation typically refers to having a seat at the negotiating table. However, I define political inclusion slightly differently than McGarry and O'Leary (2006b, 256–57). They use the term "inclusivity" to describe the quality of the institutions created by the agreement. I use it here to describe a quality of the negotiations. Although the two meanings are obviously connected, McGarry and O'Leary's sense of inclusivity differs from mine.

Civil society inclusion. Civil society encompasses a wide range of actors, both individuals and organizations, including private citizens, nongovernmental organizations (NGOs), citizens' associations, religious organizations, and worker and business unions (United Nations, n.d.; World Bank, n.d.). To test if and how the inclusion of civil society actors has an influence on referendum outcomes, I understand civil society to be composed of nonviolent organizations or groups (both civil society organizations and nongovernmental organizations) whose voluntary civic activities are separate from state institutions, but not necessarily from political parties. For example, the Northern Irish Women's Coalition is part of civil society, as it was created to represent women's and other civil society groups' interests at the GFA negotiations.

"Inclusion" is again defined broadly, from formal to informal contact between civil society groups and members of the mediation teams or representatives of the negotiating party's delegations. Drawing on Paffenholz (2014, 76–77), I consider the following forms of participation or interaction to be forms of civil society inclusion in peace negotiations, ordered from the most to the least direct: direct representation at the negotiation table; observer status at the negotiations (informal presence); participation in official consultative forums that run parallel to the negotiations; informal consultations with negotiators and mediators; high-level civil society initiatives that aim at supporting the negotiation process.[3] Paffenholz also considers any kind of mass action, such as protests, demonstrations, or petitions, and other forms of public participation, such as public hearings or public opinion polls and referendums, as civil society inclusion, whereas I do not. Public participation and civil society participation differ in some ways; the former is a more individual form of participation while the latter requires some form of public initiative and organization. Forms of public participation are better understood as a category of their own and, in fact, this book asks whether methods of civil society participation had an impact on a form of public participation—the referendums.

Agreement design. Peace agreement referendums typically ask voters whether they accept or reject the agreement reached in the negotiations. As the text of the agreement is the central focus of the referendum, it is relevant to investigate if and how the types of issues negotiated and the compromises reached during the negotiations shape the referendum campaign period and its outcome. This variable, therefore, encompasses all the negotiated issues reflected in the final agreement. These obviously vary depending on the conflict context. Regardless, negotiated settlements typically contain provisions on issues of territory, security, power-sharing institutions, or human rights.

Referendum Outcome Variables

Political party support. Research on voting behavior in referendums frequently examines whether voters follow their political

3. Inclusion of civil society in postagreement implementation mechanisms is not included here because it is not relevant to the time period being considered.

parties' or political leaders' voting preference—in other words, a voter's *political alignment*. This has already been researched for both cases (Hayes and McAllister 2001; Lordos 2008). Accordingly, I investigate the antecedent condition: whether or not political parties supported the agreement in the referendum. I call this *political (party) support*. I ask if and how the negotiation process variables shaped political leaders' and their parties' decisions to support the agreement in the referendum. By differentiating political party support from voter political party alignment, the research is sensitive to the fact that political leaders' support does not necessarily translate to votes in the referendum.

Referendum campaigns.[4] Depending on who is involved, how well organized they are, and the resources they use, campaigns can be more or less effective in influencing voters. Therefore, I look at how negotiation process conditions might have shaped the composition and strength of the "yes" and "no" campaigns. The *composition* of the campaign refers to which political or civil society actors are active in it. *Strength* is assessed by noting the resources available to them and their capacity to mobilize people.

Public information and uncertainty. As this is a qualitative study, I am concerned with whether information was *available* to the public. I will use existing quantitative studies to ascertain whether the public was informed. Given the nature of the referendums under examination, the texts of the agreements are categorized as public information. Despite

4. The period of time from the day the agreement is reached until the day the referendum is held is referred to as the *referendum campaign period* throughout the book and is not to be confused with *referendum campaign*, meaning the actual "yes" and "no" campaigns.

the public nature of an agreement, the secrecy of the negotiation process may affect how much information is available to the public before the agreement is made public. Therefore, I also care about the information available during the negotiating process.

4

The Annan Plan Experience in Cyprus

The Annan Plan Negotiations

The negotiations that produced "The Comprehensive Settlement of the Cyprus Problem," more commonly known as the "Annan Plan," were launched by Kofi Annan in 1999 soon after he was appointed UN secretary-general. The renewed effort by the UN Good Offices Mission in Cyprus to bring about an agreement between the Greek Cypriot and Turkish Cypriot leaders was headed by Annan's special representative, Álvaro de Soto, who had mediated the end to El Salvador's civil war. At the start of the negotiations, the Greek Cypriot community was represented by Glafkos Clerides, president of the Republic of Cyprus and leader of the center-right Democratic Rally (DISY), then in a coalition government with the center-left United Democrats (EDI). Rauf Denktash, the head of the center-right National Unity Party (UBP), represented the Turkish Cypriot community, as he had since UN-sponsored talks began in 1964.

In the early stages of negotiations, the relationship between the two leaders was strained, and Álvaro de Soto's initial efforts were solely focused on persuading them to meet face to face. Denktash was especially hostile to the fact that the Cypriot application to join the EU (1992) had been submitted by former Greek Cypriot President George Vassiliou. Between December 1999 and November 2000, five rounds of unsuccessful "proximity talks" were held in Geneva and New York. Pushing for a two-state solution, Denktash claimed the UN Security Council had put Turkish Cypriots at a disadvantage by recognizing the Republic of Cyprus as a legitimate state and thus not treating both parties equally (United Nations 2003, para. 24). Denktash demanded that the Turkish Republic of Northern Cyprus (TRNC)—which he had declared in 1983—be recognized as an independent state before any direct talks took place.

Finally, in December 2001 Denktash acquiesced to holding direct talks with his Greek Cypriot counterpart. The breakthrough was made possible by two events: first, the secretary-general stated publically that the "equal status" of the two parties must be recognized in the final agreement; second, Denktash's hostility to EU accession was swayed by the European Union's statement that it would accommodate any special arrangements needed to reduce economic disparities between the two sides of the island (United Nations 2003, paras. 30–32). It was then agreed between the two leaders that the talks would start with "no preconditions" and with all issues back on the table. It was also agreed that the negotiations would rely on the UN Good Offices Mission issuing draft proposals, which would be continuously revised after consultation with the parties (United Nations 2001). From then until the referendum in 2004, a total of five versions of the Annan Plan were produced in an unprecedented and concerted effort that involved UN and EU staff and numerous local teams on the island.

Other critical negotiation procedures were agreed upon in Paris in November 2002: first, the final agreement would be ratified, not by the leaders but by the people through two separate and simultaneous referendums; second, agreement would be reached by February 28, 2003, so that the referendums could take place in time for a reunited Cyprus to sign the Treaty of Accession to the EU at the Copenhagen European Council Summit in April 2003 (United Nations 2003, para. 43). Although the agreement to hold a referendum was formally based on the "concept . . . that the act of reunification of Cyprus should be an act not of the leaders but of the people on each side" (United Nations 2003, para. 72), it also aimed to bypass the need for Denktash's personal endorsement (Papapetrou 2014).

The Copenhagen summit marked an important shift in the process. Denktash declined to attend the final round of negotiations set to take place in the days preceding the summit. At the summit, with Greece threatening to veto the ten-country accession package, EU leaders accepted Cyprus as a new member. This meant that, since reunification was no longer a precondition for accession, the strategy originally devised by Holbrooke to use EU accession as an incentive for the leaders to reach a solution was no longer an option. Although the aim of reaching an agreement before accession remained the main rationale of the process, the dissipation of the EU accession incentive would surprisingly later prove to have a disastrous effect on Greek Cypriot endorsement.

Negotiations resumed in January 2003 and, shortly after, were briefly interrupted by the presidential elections in the Republic of Cyprus. Because of Clerides's advanced age (he was eighty-five at the time), he did not intend to run for another term and had, in fact, promised to support Alecos Markides's candidacy for DISY party leader (Fokaides 2014). However, pressure to bring the negotiations to a conclusion led Clerides to reconsider the timing of his retirement from politics (Fokaides 2014). Despite his campaign pledge to govern only as long as necessary to finish the Annan Plan negotiations and hold the referendums, his change of heart cost him, dividing the DISY constituency, and resulting in his (and his party's) loss.

Tassos Papadopoulos, the leader of the right-wing and traditionally nationalistic Democratic Party (DIKO), was elected president in a coalition with the more representative AKEL, the communist party led by Demetris Christofias, and the smaller, nationalistic Movement for Social Democracy (EDEK). Papadopoulos ran his presidential campaign, and won AKEL's support for his candidacy, by affirming that, like Clerides, he wanted Cyprus to join the EU as a united country, but that he would pursue a better agreement for Greek Cypriots (Faustmann 2014; Fokaides 2014; Hadjidemetriou 2014). The developments that followed, as discussed later in this chapter, show this was not his intention.

The negotiations resumed in March 2003 at The Hague, in the Netherlands. Since the leaders' endorsement was not required, the two leaders were to sign, not the agreement itself, but a two-page commitment to submit it to separate and simultaneous referendums. Papadopoulos showed a willingness to sign, as long as the gaps in federal legislation and constituent state constitutions were filled before the referendum. Denktash had fundamental objections to the plan and argued that, since the Greek Cypriot leadership had changed, negotiations should start again from square one (United Nations 2003, para. 57). Faced with a deadlock, Kofi Annan announced the end of the negotiations and held Denktash responsible.[1] The plan was left "on the table" in case the leaders showed the political will to carry it forward in the future (United Nations

1. Kofi Annan wrote to the Security Council that Denktash had failed through the years to recognize that the confrontational atmosphere of 1960 had undergone a "sea change" and was in discord with the European reality that Cyprus was about to join (United Nations 2003, para. 135).

2003, para. 60). In mid-April, the EU Treaty of Accession for the Republic of Cyprus was signed, but only by Papadopoulos.

The breakdown of the negotiations at The Hague and the consequent lost opportunity to enjoy EU membership triggered a series of demonstrations in the Turkish Cypriot community and fueled opposition to Denktash in northern Cyprus. In an attempt to appease his community, Denktash made a unilateral decision to open crossing points along the Green Line. This meant that contact between the communities on either side, which had been physically blocked since 1974, was again possible. Denktash's desperate move, however, was unable to assuage the wave of frustration that he had set in motion within his community, and his popularity continued to drop. In the 2003 TRNC parliamentary elections, "pro-solution" (the way Turkish Cypriots refer to parties opposing Denktash) Mehmet Ali Talat, leader of the Republican Turkish Party (CTP) became prime minister of the TRNC. In order to have enough seats in Parliament to form a government, the CTP formed a coalition with the Democratic Party (DP) led by Serdar Denktash, son of Rauf Denktash, who also opposed the federal solution sought in the negotiations. The DP was, however, a significantly smaller and less representative party than the CTP.

In February 2004, Annan invited the Cypriot leaders to a high-level meeting in New York. The goal was now to ensure that the negotiations would be completed by March 31, 2004, to allow the referendum to take place before May 1, 2004—the day the treaty of accession to the European Union would come into effect. It was then, Annan writes, that the Turkish Cypriot delegation (now including Talat and Serdar Denktash) proposed the novel arbitration procedure (United Nations 2004, para. 10). It was agreed by the two sides that if no finalized agreement was reached by March 22, the secretary-general would consult with the parties and "fill in the blanks" in the final plan that the leaders would put up for referendum in their respective communities (United Nations 2004, para. 12).

A complete volte-face took place in the lead-up to the final round of negotiations. Under pressure from his community, Rauf Denktash's leadership of the delegation was progressively diluted. Another problem for Denktash was that earlier in the year Recep Erdogan had become prime minister of Turkey under a pro-EU accession campaign. As Turkey's accession was contingent on a solution to the Cyprus problem, Denktash's uncooperative stance at the negotiations was inconvenient for Turkey's leadership, leading Erdogan to back Talat's pro-solution stance instead. Denktash eventually had to concede to be absent from the final round of negotiations in Bürgenstock, Switzerland, and to allow Talat to lead the Turkish Cypriot delegation.

A fourth version of the Annan Plan was then presented to the Cypriot leaders in Bürgenstock on March 27, 2004. As planned, the prime ministers of the "guarantor powers," Greece, Turkey, and the UK, as well as representatives of the European Commission for Enlargement, joined in the final round of negotiations. For the first time since 1964, the Turkish Cypriot community was not represented by its historic leader. This meant that Denktash's traditionally intransigent position gave way to Talat's commitment to deliver the Annan Plan to his community. However, suddenly, the Greek Cypriot delegation began to stall, presenting "dense and lengthy papers," insisting "on full satisfaction of its demands" (United Nations 2004, para. 22), and refusing to hold face-to-face meetings with the Turkish Cypriot delegation (United Nations 2004, paras. 31–40). A communiqué from the Press and Information Office of the Republic of Cyprus asserts that Papadopoulos refused to continue the negotiations after being pressured by the UN secretariat to negotiate new demands from Turkey (PIO 2004a), a version of events that is not corroborated by the UN. With some issues left unresolved, the agreement was submitted to the secretary-general to finalize, as was agreed upon in New York. The fifth and final version was presented to the parties on March 31, 2004.

Less than a month later, on April 24, 2004, the Annan Plan referendums were held. For the plan to be ratified, a majority "yes" vote was required from each of the communities to a question that, like the agreement itself, was extensive and detailed:

> Do you approve the Foundation Agreement with all its Annexes, as well as the constitution of the Greek Cypriot/Turkish Cypriot State and the provisions as to the laws to be in force, to bring into being a new state of affairs in which Cyprus joins the European Union united?

The results were nearly polar opposites: in the Greek Cypriot–administered Republic of Cyprus, the plan was rejected by 75.8 percent of the voters, and in TRNC, 64.9 percent of the voters accepted it (United Nations 2004, para. 72). The Greek Cypriot "no" prevented the island from unifying before EU accession. A divided Cyprus joined the European Union and, although the EU considers the whole of the territory of the island to be a member of the EU, only the Greek Cypriot community has enjoyed full membership, later also joining the euro currency area.[2]

Arbitration and Secrecy

The referendum campaign kicked off at the end of the last round of negotiations with the leaders making statements to

2. A number of EU programs have, nonetheless, financially supported economic and infrastructure development in northern Cyprus in an effort to reduce the economic gap between the communities.

international, and more importantly, local media present at Bürgenstock. Speaking to the Greek Cypriot media, Papadopoulos declared that at Bürgenstock, "Turkey added 11 new demands. . . . These demands, through the procedure of the Secretary-General using his discretion to finalize the text were met either fully or to some extent" (PIO 2004a). Papadopoulos's statements shocked the international community and set the tone for the "no" campaign in the Republic of Cyprus. The rampant government-sponsored "no" campaign drew on his statement that the agreement was biased in favor of Turkey and Turkish Cypriots and was being imposed on the Greek Cypriot community by the UN and other external powers, essentially conveying the idea that Turkey had "won" at Bürgenstock (Petasis 2004; Epaminondas 2014; Faustmann 2014; Kentas 2014). The optimistic speeches of the Turkish and Turkish Cypriot leaders, which aimed to rally support for the agreement in northern Cyprus, seemed to "confirm" this view.

Those who campaigned against the referendum in the Republic of Cyprus believed and propagated the view that, under pressure from the UK and the US, the UN was biased in favor of the Turkish side (Petasis 2004; Kentas 2014; Lillikas 2014; Tzionis 2014). To them, the Annan Plan was a biased agreement produced by a biased arbitration process. For example, Aris Petasis, an academic who actively campaigned for the "no," believed "[t]here was no mediation processes. It was a big fraud. . . . They were building the blocks to arrive at the result they had already decided" (Petasis 2004).

The arbitration process allowed Papadopoulos to claim that he had no accountability for the agreement and to campaign against it (Kaymak 2012). However, this alone does not explain why the Greek Cypriot community potentially followed their leader. It was only in his report to the Security Council in May 2004, a month after the referendum, that the secretary-general described in detail how the gaps were filled (United Nations

2004). The only potential source of this information during the referendum campaign period was the Greek Cypriot leader and delegation. The public could not judge whether there was mediator bias, as was claimed by the "no" campaign.

The lack of information needed to more critically evaluate the "no" campaign's messages on the bias and unfairness of the mediation process explains why these messages resonated in the Greek Cypriot community. A major contributing factor to this lack of information was the secrecy under which the negotiations were conducted. Holding the negotiations in complete secrecy was an important part of Álvaro de Soto's mediation strategy, particularly during the early stages of the process. No reports by the secretary-general on the Good Offices Mission were issued between June 1999 and April 2003, during which time the Security Council was only orally briefed (United Nations 2003, para. 2). Arguing for the advantages of secret negotiations, Álvaro de Soto stated in an interview in 2002: "Just as there exists the fog of war in which the first victim is the truth, there should exist the fog of diplomacy, or the fog of Good Offices, in which the truth should only come out in the end result" (De Soto 2002, 89). This secrecy came back to haunt him in the referendum.

Accustomed to being scapegoated by the Cypriot leaders throughout their long years of mission in Cyprus, UN Good Offices Mission personnel were reserved when talking to the media about the negotiations. Cypriot journalists on both sides of the island relied on politicians as the main source of information (Kutay 2014; Özuslu 2014; Pavlowitch 2014). The secrecy of the process, however, also allowed political leaders to withhold or give false information. Marios Epaminondas, who campaigned for the "yes" in the Republic of Cyprus and became an active member of Greek Cypriot civil society after the Annan Plan experience, is adamant that it allowed politicians to "keep the people ignorant about what was being negotiated," to "blame the other side for everything that goes wrong," and to criticize the UN mediators (Epaminondas 2014). Similarly, Maria Hadjipavlou, an academic, civil society activist, and "yes" campaigner, believes there was a lack of information on the main issues being discussed in the negotiations. This prevented public debate and discussion in the Greek Cypriot community from starting before the referendum campaign began (Hadjipavlou 2014). The physical separation between the two communities made it even easier for Greek Cypriot politicians to withhold or give false information; no counter-perspective from the other side of the Green Line reached their community (Epaminondas 2014; Pavlowitch 2014; Pericleous 2014).

The lack of availability of meaningful information and, hence, the lack of any reason for debate in the Greek Cypriot community set the stage for a referendum campaign period permeated by disinformation and propaganda. Papadopoulos's statements resonated with the Greek Cypriot community's fears; for historical reasons, the two Cypriot communities were (and still are) distrustful of external actors' involvement in the Cyprus problem. More specifically, the Zurich-London Agreements that created the 1960 Republic of Cyprus were agreed upon by the UK, Greece, and Turkey, and are largely seen as having been "imposed" on the two Cypriot communities. In addition to rehashing the colonial trauma, Papadopoulos's campaign rhetoric relied on the revival of Greek Cypriot nationalism and victimhood. Together, these two aspects of the "no" campaign atrophied public space for the discussion of the implications of a "no" vote (Anastasiou 2008, 144–45).

In addition, the state apparatus and the media were mobilized and misused to misconstrue Papadopoulos's rhetoric in the very early stages of the referendum campaign. Kosta

Pavlowitch, journalist and editor of the *Cyprus Mail* at the time, witnessed Greek Cypriot journalists at Bürgenstock "not cross-checking sources and running stories on leaks that were made in order to undermine the process" (Pavlowitch 2014). In her analysis of the Greek Cypriot media reports on the Annan Plan during the referendum campaign, Yiouli Taki (2009, 187–88) shows how television broadcasts relied on distorted information coming from unnamed sources and presented uncorrected misinterpretations of the Plan's provisions favoring the "no" campaign. In addition, with the exception of *Politis*, *Alithia*, and the *Cyprus Mail*, the majority of the Greek Cypriot printed press supported the "no" vote in the referendum campaign.

The climate was such that the otherwise media-shy UN mission was propelled into action in the days leading to the referendum. At first—and already too late to overturn the tide—Álvaro de Soto wrote to Papadopoulos asking that he publicly dispel misinformation being given by government officials on the negative implications of the Annan Plan for civil servants' job security (De Soto 2004), as this had bolstered teachers' union support for the "no" campaign. Papadopoulos categorically refused: "You ask me publicly to state through the media that the public and the civil service are being misinformed. I do not believe that your assignment gives you any legitimate right to ask me or suggest what my position should or not be" (Papadopoulos 2004). After this exchange of letters, Álvaro de Soto was prevented from speaking on the state-funded Greek Cypriot television channel CYBC (De Soto 2004). Reporting to the Security Council after the referendum, Kofi Annan regretted that "[t]he efforts of the United Nations to provide explanations and clarifications about the plan to the public at large were hampered by the media climate on the island" (United Nations 2004, para. 71).

As the Greek Cypriot experience shows, political leaders' support can shape referendum campaigns and affect referendum results. An agreement that is not endorsed by important political figures in the community—and especially by those who negotiated it—will naturally struggle to get support (Drath 2004; Kaymak 2012). However, Denktash campaigned for the "no" side using rhetoric similar to that used by Papadopoulos (Bryant 2004), but the majority of Turkish Cypriots voted in favor of the plan. Why did Papadopoulos succeed while Denktash failed?

The Turkish Cypriot leader's position had less effect on Turkish Cypriot voters for a number of reasons. An important factor was the engagement of the community during the negotiations. Negotiation secrecy led to a poorly engaged and misinformed Greek Cypriot public; however, this was not true of the Turkish Cypriot community. By the time the Bürgenstock negotiations took place, the community was largely mobilized and collectively organized to support the negotiations and the Annan Plan in the referendum. In fact, negotiations entered public discussions as early as 2000. Sener Elcil, leader of the Turkish Cypriot Teachers Union (KTOS) and an influential figure in Turkish Cypriot civil society, recalls that, eager to put an end to its isolation and dependency on Turkey by joining the EU, a section of the community grew impatient with Denktash's negotiating behavior (Elcil 2014; Özuslu 2014). Dozens of civil society organizations, business groups, and left-wing pro-solution political parties came together to create the This Country Is Ours platform with the initial aim of putting pressure on Denktash to negotiate.

The This Country Is Ours platform became the arena for close cooperation between the pro-solution, leftist political party leaders and civil society, particularly Ali Talat and Mustafa Akinci, leader of the Communal Liberation Party (TKP) and then of the Peace and Democracy Movement (PDM) upon its creation in 2003 (Akinci 2014; Elcil 2014; Talat 2014).[3] To Talat, mobilizing the community between December 2002 and the referendum was crucial to pressuring Denktash to withdraw from the delegation and not be present at the last round of negotiations at Bürgenstock. During this period, Talat recalls, "Every day and every night there was something for the Annan Plan" (Talat 2014). Furthermore, unlike the media in the Republic of Cyprus, the majority of Turkish Cypriot media was supportive of the Annan Plan. Sami Özuslu, who was working at the time for SIM, a private radio station popular during the referendum, explained that the media cooperated with politicians, academics, and civil society organizations to inform and engage the community in a discussion of the benefits and shortcomings of the plan, especially after its release in 2003 (Özuslu 2014).

While secrecy handicapped public debate on the Annan Plan in the Greek Cypriot community and created a vacuum allowing the insertion of disinformation and the nationalistic rhetoric of the "no" campaign, the north was different. An alternative discourse was already operating in the Turkish Cypriot community.

Differences in Political Inclusion

The two Cypriot communities had been represented by their elected leaders since the UN-led negotiations started in 1964. As a result, the respective delegations were formed by the governing party or coalition of parties in power at a given time. This had important consequences for the negotiations. First,

3. For a more detailed account of the political transformation and civil society mobilization in northern Cyprus during the Annan Plan negotiations, see Kizilyürek (2012).

two times during the Annan Plan process, negotiations were delayed or interrupted by election periods. Second, the election of new leaders resulted in shifts in the positions of each side. When the 2003 elections led to a more pro-solution and cooperative Turkish Cypriot negotiation party, a more conservative and less compromising Greek Cypriot party countered it. Third, the election of new leaders hindered compromises made by their predecessors, or even took negotiations back to square one, as Denktash tried to do when Papadopoulos was elected.

The political parties that were not in power were excluded from the negotiations and were formally briefed by the delegations on each side in different ways. The Greek Cypriot presidents convened National Council meetings to inform and receive advice from all political parties and former presidents, while Denktash's delegation prepared reports that were made available to the political parties in the Parliament in the TRNC.

The politically exclusive nature of the negotiations affected political party support in the referendum campaigns in the south. Those who negotiated the agreement did not support it and the strong anti-Annan Plan sentiment that developed thereafter incurred significant political costs for the parties who supported it. Papadopoulos' public position against the Annan Plan at Bürgenstock determined the positioning of other political parties. Within the coalition in power, while it was not problematic for the nationalistic EDEK to follow DIKO's lead, AKEL struggled to maintain the party's pro-solution orientation. Its leader, Demetris Christofias, was faced with the decision of either maintaining support for the "yes," thus jeopardizing the coalition government, or switching the party's vote to "no," thus seeming to support DIKO's turn to nationalism (Anastasiou 2008, 164). Trapped between a rock and a hard place, the AKEL leader made a desperate move.

Christofias asked the Security Council to guarantee that Turkey would respect the security provisions of the Annan Plan, and to delay the referendum by six months to allow more time for the community to understand the merits of the agreement. The efforts of the communist party were ironically derailed by Russia's veto of the resolution, presumably due to DIKO's secret persuasion. In the end AKEL supported a "soft no" in the referendum, which was nonetheless a significant departure from its traditionally pro-solution stance.

In Clerides's DISY, the decision on whether the party would support the agreement was divisive. Despite party polls indicating that the "no" vote would reach 60 percent, DISY's leaders decided to support the "yes" vote. This decision was influenced by Clerides's position as the party's historic leader, former president of the Republic, and negotiator of one of the first versions of the plan (Fokaides 2014). However, the party members were split, with some deciding to abandon the party and/or to campaign for the "no" vote. As a result, the party's "yes" campaign was significantly weakened. As Fokaides (spokesperson for DISY in 2014) explains, "DISY was careful not to impose the leadership's position"; consequently, "the support for the Plan was framed as a recommendation." Due to the party's internal divisions, "it was not possible to develop a full-fledged campaign" (Fokaides 2014).

Under the pressure created by Papadopoulos's strong rhetoric against the agreement and the growing negative public opinion, AKEL's support for the "no" vote and DISY's split meant that the "yes" received little political support in the south. In the end, only two parties campaigned for the "yes" vote: DISY and the smaller center-left United Democrats (EDI). Although they collaborated in a few campaign events, due to the different tones in which they supported the agreement, the two parties essentially led independent campaigns

(Hadjidemetriou 2014; Vassiliou 2014). In contrast, the "no" vote had DIKO, EDEK, AKEL to a lesser extent, and DISY dissenters campaigning for it.

A different reality developed in the Turkish Cypriot community, where opposition political parties were comparatively more included in the negotiations. Denktash's intransigence and the community's uprising against him led the UN Good Offices Mission to seek contact with the leaders of left-wing pro-solution political parties. In effect, Talat and Akinci were informally consulted by the UN Good Offices Mission personnel even before Talat was elected prime minister in 2003 (Akinci 2014; Talat 2014). Akinci[4] met with Álvaro de Soto at de Soto's request to talk, not necessarily about the details of the agreement but to get "a general understanding of where the negotiations stood" (Akinci 2014). Talat had a bolder and more substantive view: "Actually, the opposition was negotiating the Plan with the UN instead of the Turkish Cypriot official leader in 2002" (Talat 2014).

While in the Greek Cypriot community, the political parties outside the negotiations waited until the final version of the agreement was made public to announce their position; in the Turkish Cypriot community, the political parties' positions were known much earlier. In fact, the pro-Annan Plan/EU election campaign led Talat's CTP to victory in 2003 (Hatay 2004). A split similar to the one in DISY beset Serdar Denktash's Democratic Party, leading him to expel prominent party members three days before the referendum (PIO 2004b). The party's involvement in the Annan Plan negotiations challenged its traditional hardline stance against the

4. In 2015, more than ten years after the Annan Plan referendum, Akinci was elected president in the TRNC.

federal solution enshrined in the agreement. The party eventually adopted a "soft no" stance during the campaign and advised constituents to decide for themselves.

In effect, the "no" campaign in the Turkish Cypriot community was led by the UBP, Denktash's former party, and elements of the Turkish military present on the island (Özuslu 2014). In the same style as the "yes" campaign, the "no" campaign organized demonstrations and distributed pamphlets door to door. However, as Talat explained, the "yes" campaign was more effective than the "no" campaign because it was based on long-term continuous mobilization at the grassroots level (Talat 2014). Those in the "yes" campaign say it didn't just happen between Bürgenstock and the day of the referendum; it was a continued effort that started as early as 2002 or even 2000 (Akinci 2014; Elcil 2014; Talat 2014).

Civil Society Inclusion and Mobilization

UN mediation in Cyprus never formally included civil society groups, and the Annan Plan negotiations were no exception. However, there were informal forms of inclusion for the Turkish Cypriot community. As already described, the negotiations prompted the community to take action, and civil society groups supported the negotiations. As part of these efforts, in August 2002, the This Country Is Ours platform devised a declaration of support for the negotiations and sent it to the secretary-general. "The Common Vision of the Turkish Cypriot Civil Society" expressed its signatories' support for the solution envisioned in the Annan Plan and called for agreement to be reached before the December Copenhagen Summit, where the EU would accept Cyprus's membership candidacy. A total of eighty-six civil society groups, prosolution parties, and unions signed the document.

Through the efforts of This Country Is Ours, civil society leaders in the Turkish Cypriot community participated in informal consultations with UN personnel, including Álvaro de Soto, while the negotiations were in progress (Elcil 2014; Erel 2014). The Turkish Cypriot Chamber of Commerce served as the meeting point. Ali Erel, head of the Chamber of Commerce between 2001 and 2005, attests: "We had Mr. De Soto visiting us very often, and then Thomas Weston, the representative of the USA was speaking to us as well, and all the ambassadors of the member states." The civil society groups and opposition party leaders who participated in these meetings informed the mediators of "the communal point of view" and were "helping them, in a way, to recognize the needs of the people better" (Erel 2014).

In his reports to the Security Council, Kofi Annan rarely mentions civil society. However, the following citation, referring to the period before the Copenhagen summit and, therefore, before Talat's election, confirms that the input from civil society leaders in the north was acknowledged and, in fact, influenced the agreement's drafting. The comment relates to a period when Denktash was refusing to negotiate: "Regrettably, the substantive input from the Turkish Cypriot side was extremely general and largely conceptual—leaving the United Nations to seek inspiration for concrete improvements from concerns publicly voiced by a cross section of Turkish Cypriot civil society" (United Nations 2003, para. 45).

In the referendum, an umbrella "yes" campaign was a natural continuation of the activities of This Country Is Ours. The same unions, organizations and political parties who organized and mobilized to influence the negotiations cooperated in leading a strongly organized "yes" campaign. Between December 2002 and March 2004, the This Country Is Ours organized demonstrations, rallies, and "peace fires," among other activities, where people linked to the platform gathered locals to talk about the Annan Plan (Elcil 2014; Talat 2014). In addition, the organization created and distributed pamphlets explaining the agreement in a question-and-answer format with 100 questions.

The same contact between mediation team members and civil society groups did not take place in the Greek Cypriot community. In the south, civil society did not engage with the negotiations to the same extent, nor did it become particularly mobilized during the referendum campaign period. In fact, only a handful of NGOs involved in peacebuilding activities mobilized in support of the negotiations as part of their reconciliation work in Cyprus (based on statements by Faustmann, 2014; Hadjipavlou, 2014; Potier, 2014). The "yes" campaign was loosely organized and mainly enacted—aside from EDI, and DISY's lackluster support—by individuals and NGOs fostering bicommunal activities (Epaminondas 2014). "Yes" campaigners in the south also had trouble reaching the Greek Cypriot community due to the insidious "demonization" of "yes" campaigners and the "yes" vote (Epaminondas 2014; Hadjidemetriou 2014; Hadjipavlou 2014; Papapetrou 2014). Papapetrou (2014), who campaigned for the "yes" with EDI, and many others were accused by politicians in the "no" camp of being "traitors" and "the servants of foreign actors." Maria Hadjipavlou (2014), who also campaigned for the "yes" vote, says, "The 'yes' became the unpatriotic voice, the voice of the traitors." The more influential figures campaigning for the "yes" were threatened and persecuted.

In the Turkish Cypriot community, no civil society groups were involved in the "no" campaign. This was different in the Greek Cypriot community. Although the Orthodox Church of Cyprus did not engage in campaigning activities, the archbishop publicly expressed support for the "no" and used mass to spread those views. The Pancyprian Citizens Movement played a more active part in the "no" campaign by organizing events and distributing campaign materials (Kentas 2014). The group had been working to mobilize the Greek Cypriot community against the Annan Plan since 2002 but did not do so explicitly until Bürgenstock.

While civil society groups in the Turkish Cypriot community coordinated to influence the negotiations and to be included, among Greek Cypriots, the negotiations remained an issue of the political elites. The collaborative effort to push for inclusion and the ongoing support easily evolved into a strong and well-organized "yes" campaign in the north. Similar efforts were too little and too late in the south.

A Comprehensive Agreement

Officially titled "The Comprehensive Settlement of the Cyprus Problem," the Annan Plan provided for the foundation of the United Cyprus Republic, a federal state with two constituent states of equal political status (United Nations 2004, para. 42). Drawing on the Swiss and Belgian Constitutions, the Annan Plan proposed a state with a single international personality and sovereignty, where partition and secession were prohibited, but without hierarchy between federal and constituent state lawmaking (United Nations 2003, paras. 74–76). Again inspired by the Swiss Constitution, the plan provided for a Presidential Council with a rotating presidency, whereby the presidency would alternate between the election of a Greek Cypriot and a Turkish Cypriot (United Nations 2004, para. 44). Furthermore, the plan provided for a gradual lifting of limitations on the freedom of settlement on the island and a scheme of incentives, compensations, and bonds for displaced or dispossessed landowners who would need to give up their properties in the other constituent state to current occupants (United Nations 2004, para. 48–50, 55). As this was less favorable to Greek Cypriots, it was compensated by a territorial adjustment; the UK would cede the territory occupied by its Sovereign Base Areas mainly to the Greek Cypriot constituent state (United Nations 2003, para. 116). The plan laid the groundwork for a longer transitional period in the application of the *aquis communautaire* in the Turkish Cypriot constituent state to favor the growth of its fragile economy (United Nations 2004, para. 57). On security issues, Greece, Turkey, and the UK would remain as guarantor powers. The number of foreign troops present on the island would be gradually reduced to symbolic numbers, even in the event of Turkey's accession to the EU (United Nations 2004, para. 47). A UN peacekeeping operation would monitor the agreement's implementation (United Nations 2004, para. 45).

Since the referendum, scholars from each of the communities in Cyprus have scrutinized the merits and shortcomings of the Annan Plan (see, for example, Coufoudakis and Kyriakides 2004; Moulakis 2007; Loizides 2009). At the root of the debate is the question of whether it represented a balanced and fair outcome to both communities. I take a somewhat different approach and question the role the provisions of the agreement actually played in the referendum result. I ask, first, if they were fundamental to political leaders' and parties' decisions on whether to support the agreement in the referendum and, second, whether they played a more direct role in shaping voters' decision-making.

Although both Papadopoulos and Denktash claimed the Annan Plan did not accommodate their interests, whether covertly or openly, both were actually unwilling to support it from the get go. Tassos Tzionis, a delegate on Papadopoulos's negotiating team, believes the Greek Cypriot leader, as well as DIKO, did not support the Annan Plan because the UN Good Offices Mission failed to create an agreement that sufficiently addressed Greek Cypriot interests: "We never accepted Turkish guarantees and the continuation of the stationing of Turkish troops on the island and bi-zonality as interpreted by the UN. . . . When we accepted a bi-zonal and bi-communal federation, we meant something else" (Tzionis 2014). In fact, less than two weeks before the referendum, in a tearful televised speech, Papadopoulos pleaded to the Greek Cypriot community to vote "no," arguing that the agreement had "dangerous obscurities" in the area of security, and that the presence of Turkish troops on the island would promote Turkish "colonization." To this he added, "With the final Annan Plan Cypriots have not been satisfied, however Turkey's pursuit to control and dominate Cyprus has been fully met" (PIO 2004a).

These accounts suggest that Papadopoulos and DIKO did not support the Annan Plan because it did not satisfy the interests of the community. However, Papadopoulos likely never intended to reach an agreement that he could "sell" to the Greek Cypriot community. Among those involved in the Annan Plan negotiations, there is a common perception that Papadopoulos and his team misled everyone at the table into believing he would support the agreement (AKEL Politician 2014; Demetriou 2014; Hadjidemetriou 2014; Papapetrou 2014; Talat 2014; Vassiliou 2014). Former president George Vassiliou and EDI politician Takis Hadjidemetriou, who negotiated the provisions of the agreement related to EU harmonization, were surprised and felt "cheated" when Papadopoulos announced he was against the agreement after Bürgenstock (Hadjidemetriou 2014; Vassiliou 2014). In fact, Greek Cypriot politicians widely believe Papadopoulos was unwilling to agree on a solution that would not provide for a unitary state where Greek Cypriots would enjoy majority rule, even though he led all to believe that he supported the creation of a bizonal and bicommunal federation. Denktash's intransigence, some argue, allowed Papadopoulos to maintain a cooperative appearance during the negotiations (AKEL Politician 2014; Hadjidemetriou 2014). Arbitration further enabled Papadopoulos by removing the need to bargain for a compromise solution. It instead placed the delegations' focus on persuading the mediation team to support their positions and created an incentive for the parties to cease presenting more compromising positions on issues. As Talat explained, "we were not negotiating with the Greek Cypriots . . . we were trying to persuade the UN to take our part." Consequently, "we were keeping our positions at an acceptable level, not demanding too much, but also not compromising easily, whereas if the negotiations would have been between the two sides . . . we would have had to compromise" (Talat 2014).

The Greek Cypriot parties who supported the Annan Plan believed it was not perfect, but its deficiencies could be addressed after the referendum. For example, Panayiotis Demetriou, deputy leader of DISY during Clerides's presidency, says DISY leaders had concerns about the implementation of the Annan Plan, but believed it could be improved during its implementation (Demetriou 2014). As noted above, DISY and EDI's decisions to support the Annan Plan in the referendum had to do with issues of accountability, because they were part of the negotiations.

It is unsatisfying to explain the Greek Cypriot political parties' decision to support the agreement based only on whether or not it accommodated their interests. The fact that many announced their position on the referendum later in the campaign further attests that those outside the negotiations felt pressured to position themselves against the agreement because of the anti–Annan Plan propaganda following Bürgenstock. The text of the agreement might not have been the central cause. In this sense, the fact that the Annan Plan did not require the Cypriot leaders' signature and endorsement to be ratified was a significant hindrance to gathering political support in the referendum.

Like Papadopoulos, Denktash purportedly did not support the Annan Plan because, according to his political advisor Ergün Olgun, "he believed that the provisions in the agreement did not make it sustainable in the long run for the two sides" (Olgun 2014). Olgun says Denktash believed residential properties should belong to the communities administrating the territory, but this was not part of the Annan Plan. In addition, he was not satisfied with the economic inequality safeguards (Olgun 2014). However, unlike Papadopoulos, Denktash did not negotiate the final version of the Annan Plan. As noted above, by the end, Talat was leading the negotiation team with Turkey's support (Talat 2014), with Serdar Denktash's DP on the negotiating team, and with the longer-term support of Akinci and his New Democracy Movement.

While the text of an agreement will shape political leaders' and parties' support in a referendum, as put forward earlier in this book, its impact on voting behaviors depends on how well informed voters are about its content and potential implications. The core section of the Annan Plan was an almost 200-page-long complex juridical text that Kofi Annan describes as a "truly comprehensive proposal" (United Nations 2003, para. 61). The extensive and complex nature of the agreement made it difficult for the public to grasp fully. This was especially problematic in the Greek Cypriot community. Since then, Álvaro de Soto has expressed the view that "Greek Cypriots had not fully understood, from lack of explanation from their leaders, what a federal system involved" (De Soto 2012, 402). Plus, Epaminondas, who campaigned for the "yes," says he faced resistance when he attempted to distribute booklets explaining the Annan Plan.[5] He states, "They (Greek Cypriots) were positive that it was a bad Plan and . . . they were not ready to listen to any other opinion" (Epaminondas 2014).

5. The booklet was published by the Peace Research Institute Oslo; see Alexiou et al. (2003).

Those who campaigned for the "yes" vote in the Republic of Cyprus believe that the one-month period between Bürgenstock and the referendum was insufficient to inform the public or lead a sufficient public debate (Fokaides 2014; Hadjipavlou 2014). Yet this time limit is not seen to have negatively affected the results in the north (Elcil 2014; Talat 2014). Here, a more engaged community with a more collectively mobilized civil society and media encouraged public debate on the negotiations for longer, having started sooner. The Turkish Cypriot community generally understood the document because it was discussed extensively, particularly on the radio and in newspapers before the referendum (Akinci 2014; Elcil 2014; Özuslu 2014; Talat 2014). Sami Özuslu, who hosted a TV show dedicated to the Annan Plan, explains that the media cooperated with politicians and civil society in informing the community. Politicians and academics read and analyzed the Annan Plan on the radio and in newspapers after the third version was made public in 2003 following the collapse of the negotiations at The Hague (Özuslu 2014). Scholars who have written on the Turkish Cypriot perspectives and experiences in the referendum also say Turkish Cypriots were informed voters (Bryant 2004; Kaymak 2009), and this was a direct consequence of the dissemination of information starting in 2002 (Hatay 2004; Kaymak 2009, 143).

Because public debates were held earlier and civil society was more engaged, the Turkish Cypriot community was more familiar with the content of the agreement at the time of the referendum than the Greek Cypriot community. The lack of public information and debate in the latter community suggests that Greek Cypriots were more influenced by political party support and campaign cues, which were dominated by "no" voices and slogans. Public opinion surveys have found that the victory of the "no" vote in the Greek Cypriot community conveyed people's dissatisfaction with specific provisions of the

Annan Plan, such as those relating to Turkish military presence on the island, financial, property issues, or providing citizenship to Turkish settlers (Georgiades 2007; Lordos 2008). However, they do not consider when or how those opinions were formed and therefore do not account for the possibility that respondents' opinions might have been influenced or "learned" during the campaign. While some studies ask whether Greek Cypriots were informed voters (Lordos 2004, 2009), findings are based on respondents' self-assessments. Respondents are not asked about the sources of their information.

A Tale of Two Stories

The physical and psychological separation of the two Cypriot communities not only allowed very different referendum results but also permitted two different negotiation and referendum experiences. The Annan Plan referendum is, in fact, not only a case of rejection of the peace agreement, but also one of approval. Therefore, it was sensible to consider the influence of the negotiation process not only on the Greek Cypriot rejection or low support for the Annan Plan, but also on Turkish Cypriot approval. Surprisingly, there were differences in mediator behaviors toward each of the communities and in political and civic engagement during the negotiations.

The Annan Plan mediation process is an especially rich case in terms of the range of mediation strategies and unique in allowing a hybridization of mediation and arbitration. As mentioned earlier in this book, the different aspects of the UN's mediation strategy are frequently cited in explanations of the failure of the Annan Plan initiative (Drath 2004; Lordos 2004, Michael 2007; Kaymak 2012). Although the mediation strategy certainly contributed to the rejection of the agreement, previous assessments do not fully explain how it shaped the campaign period or the voting behaviors. President Papadopoulos was not held sufficiently accountable for the agreement and could therefore come out strongly against it, but this does not explain why Greek Cypriots were convinced by the "no" campaign's arguments. The secrecy of the negotiation process is key to understanding how Papadopoulos's claim of unaccountability was perceived as legitimate. In fact, the mediation strategies became part of "no" supporters' arguments; they made the case that the Annan Plan was a biased imposition from abroad and a bad outcome for Greek Cypriots, and they questioned the UN's credibility as a mediator. The campaign period was dominated by a "no" campaign headed by political leaders who capitalized on the lack of information available to the public to discredit the mediation process. In the end, the arbitration procedure allowed political leaders to appear unaccountable, and secrecy predisposed a poorly engaged and ill-informed community to follow the cues of the strong and highly politically backed "no" campaign.

The negotiation process was comparatively more inclusive in the Turkish Cypriot community than in the Greek Cypriot community. The lack of political and civic inclusion meant voter education in the south did not really begin until the start of the referendum campaign period—and the tone for this was set by Papadopoulos's negative appraisal.

Of course, negotiation process conditions alone do not explain the difference in support between the two communities. The prospect of EU membership was crucial to the "yes" vote in the Turkish Cypriot community at a time of economic turmoil (Bahcheli 2004; Lordos 2008). Also contributing to the "yes" in the north was Erdogan's support for the Annan Plan; this is seen to have increased the "yes" vote in the Turkish migrant population. The fact that the agreement provided the possibility of citizenship in the new federal republic to a considerable portion of these settlers caused many to vote "yes" (Talat 2014). Yet the Annan Plan experience triggered an upsurge of political and civic mobilization that affected the negotiations themselves and shaped the referendum experience in northern Cyprus. Such an explanation goes further than existing arguments that Turkish Cypriots supported the Annan Plan because EU accession would end their decade-long isolation and their economic dependency on Turkey. While this is true, we cannot ignore that the implementation of the Annan Plan also meant that Turkish Cypriots would have to live together with Greek Cypriots, from whom they historically fear domination. A simplistic explanation of the Turkish Cypriot vote based on the promise of EU accession alone also minimizes the remarkable mass mobilization in northern Cyprus in support, first for the negotiations, and then for the resulting agreement in the referendum.

The same applies to the claim that Greek Cypriots did not support the Annan Plan because accession to the EU was given to the community with or without reunification. Having accession conditional to reunification might have worked as an incentive for Papadopoulos to support the Annan Plan and shaped the referendum campaign in an entirely different way. Yet the absence of this incentive cannot explain the outcome in the community on its own.

In the end, for the Greek Cypriot community, the Annan Plan referendum was essentially an undemocratic experience aided by the exclusionist nature of the negotiations, but the opposite was the case for the Turkish Cypriot community. While the secrecy and the lack of public debate left an uninformed and disengaged Greek Cypriot public to rely on political leaders' cues to make a voting decision, a much greater and much earlier engagement of opposition parties and civil society groups with the negotiations in the Turkish Cypriot community mobilized support for the Annan Plan.

5

The Good Friday Agreement Experience in Northern Ireland

The Good Friday Agreement Negotiations

The negotiations that led to the Good Friday Agreement took place in Belfast over two years—from June 1996 to April 1998—at the Castle Buildings in Stormont, a Belfast suburb. Known as the All-Party or Multi-Party Talks, the negotiations were made possible—and were shaped—by the negotiation attempts of the British and Irish governments in preceding decades. For this reason, authors use different starting points when describing the process that led to the GFA. The signing of the Sunningdale Agreement in 1973 and the Anglo-Irish Agreement in 1985 are commonly recognized as starting the process. Although the contents of the GFA negotiations were affected by the preceding agreements, the negotiation process was markedly different in one important aspect. The failure of the Sunningdale power-sharing experience of 1973–74 brought with it an important realization for the British and Irish governments: any future agreement could easily be spoiled if the political parties associated with the paramilitary groups continued to be excluded (Horowitz 2002, 194, 203; McGarry and O'Leary 2006b, 262).

The decommissioning of the paramilitaries and their respective pledges to reject violence became preconditions for this more inclusive approach, and the first source of friction. The Unionist political parties and the British government demanded that the paramilitaries turn in their arms before the political parties associated with them were allowed to negotiate, but the PIRA refused to do so. The disagreement over the conditions of inclusion led to the first stalemate of the peace process and propelled United States involvement. The Irish community in the United States had grown increasingly dissatisfied with the Republic of Ireland's moderate position on Northern Ireland and lobbied to get the US involved in the peace process (O'Dowd 2008; Cochrane, Baser, and Swain 2009).

The Clinton administration had a major impact on breaking the stalemate caused by the decommissioning issue. An International Body on Arms Decommissioning was set up, with US Senator George Mitchell, special envoy to Northern Ireland, as chairman (Fitzduff 2002, 128). The report of the Mitchell Commission, as it became known, set the ground rules for the Good Friday Agreement negotiations. The report recommended that a simultaneous and parallel decommissioning of the republican and loyalist paramilitaries take place alongside the peace negotiations (art. 34). Importantly, it also recommended that the negotiations take place in an elected body (art. 56). Unionists and the British government seized this recommendation and insisted that elections be held to determine which political parties would participate. Republicans regarded this as a show of intransigence and a stalling tactic. The disagreement eventually led the PIRA to break the ceasefire in February 1996 with the bombing of Canary Wharf, London (McGrattan 2010, 147, 148).

Despite this setback, elections for the Northern Ireland Forum for Political Dialogue, also known as the Peace Forum, were held on May 30, 1996. Since Sinn Féin[1], the political arm of the PIRA and the fourth largest political party in Northern Ireland at the time, would undoubtedly get seats, the British government designed the electoral system to guarantee that the smaller loyalist parties would also be able to participate (Mitchell 1999, 43). Five seats were marked for each Westminster Parliamentary constituency of Northern Ireland, under the D'Hondt method of party-list proportional representation, with an extra two seats for each of the ten parties with the most votes. As a result, ten political parties were elected to negotiate the peace agreement.

The Ulster Unionist Party (UUP), headed by David Trimble, represented the largest Unionist political party at the time and thus gained the most seats. The UUP was reluctant to accept any form of power-sharing with the Nationalist community, especially with Sinn Féin, or to allow the involvement of the Irish government in Northern Ireland politics. The second largest Unionist party, founded by Presbyterian Church leader Reverend Ian Paisley, was the Democratic Unionist Party (DUP). The DUP pursued a harder political line by advocating the dominance of Unionism and the Ulster identity in Northern Ireland. The DUP and the smaller United Kingdom Unionist Party (UKUP), led by Robert McCartney, were ideologically resistant to power-sharing.

As a result of the electoral system, the Progressive Unionist Party (PUP) (linked to the Ulster Volunteer Force and Red Hand Commandos) and the Ulster Democratic Party (UDP) (linked to the Ulster Defence Association) also joined the negotiations. Because they drew on loyalist paramilitary

1. Although Sinn Féin is widely believed to be the political arm of the PIRA, this has always been denied by its leaders.

constituencies, the release of prisoners became an important issue for these parties when the topic was introduced by Sinn Féin later in the negotiations. Additionally, unlike the remaining Unionist parties, the PUP and the UDP accepted Sinn Féin's future participation in government (Horowitz 2002, 208).

On the Nationalist flank, the Social Democratic and Labour Party (SDLP) and Sinn Féin both gained seats in the Forum. Led by John Hume, the SDLP was the largest Nationalist political party at the time. Born out of the civil rights movement of the 1970s, the party professed a more moderate version of Irish nationalism (McGrattan 2010, 39). SDLP supporters were, nonetheless, divided over those who supported unity with the Republic of Ireland was the long-term goal, and those who preferred to remain in the United Kingdom. Sinn Féin represented the more radical republican desire for immediate unity with Ireland and supported the need for the armed struggle against British rule (Ruane and Todd 1996, 67,70). By the start of the GFA negotiations, however, the party's position had softened and was articulated as part of an Irish peace initiative aimed at removing the need for violence (Adams 1997).

Two bicommunal and moderate—yet organically different—political parties were also elected to the forum: the older Alliance Party and the new civil society–led Northern Ireland Women's Coalition (NIWC). The Alliance Party was founded in April 1970 by members of the Catholic and Protestant communities who were against political sectarianism (Close 2014). Promoting the unity of the two Christian Churches and gathering support across the two communities, the Alliance Party supported a pragmatic union with Britain within a power-sharing arrangement (Ruane and Todd 1996, 60–61). The Alliance Party's capacity to communicate with both

Unionists and Nationalists rendered party leader John Alderdice and deputy leader Seamus Close key participants in the negotiations (Mitchell 1999, 44).

The Northern Ireland Women's Coalition was a new party set up as part of a civil society initiative to participate in the negotiations. Although the original aim was to have women participate in the negotiations to represent and advocate for women's issues, the party's negotiating agenda broadened as the negotiations progressed. The party felt that the negotiations should focus on more than power and paramilitary issues and brought human rights and other issues to the table (Kilmurray 2014; Morrice 2014). The treatment of the victims of paramilitary violence, the integration of former prisoners, integrated education, and the participation of civil society in political life were some of the issues they targeted.

Although the elections to the Peace Forum determined which parties would negotiate the agreement, the negotiation process which eventually produced the GFA did not, in fact, take place in the Peace Forum. While the Peace Forum discussed some of the issues under negotiation and offered proposals to the main negotiations, the agreement was negotiated between the delegations of the parties in the All-Party Talks. In addition to the representatives of the Northern Ireland political parties, representatives of the British and Irish governments were present in plenary sessions.

All political parties agreed upon the procedural rules of the negotiations before the first session of the All-Party Talks. The negotiations would be based on the principle that "nothing is agreed until everything is agreed" and have a three-strand structure: strand one covered the negotiations between political parties of Northern Ireland on relationships within Northern Ireland; strand two covered the relationship between Northern Ireland and the Republic of Ireland; and strand three dealt with the relationship between the British and Irish governments. A triple-lock system[2] would be used to ratify the agreement: first it would have to receive the support of the political parties in the negotiations; then it would have to be endorsed by the British Parliament and the Irish government and Parliament; lastly, it would have to be supported by a majority of the people of Northern Ireland in a referendum.

The first session of the talks took place on June 10, 1996, at the Castle Buildings in Stormont, Belfast. After chairing the International Body on Arms Decommissioning, George Mitchell was invited by the British and Irish governments to chair the plenary sessions of the All-Party Talks (Mitchell 1999, 45). Since the loyalist paramilitaries had maintained their cease-fire, the political parties associated with them joined the negotiations. Because the PIRA had breached the cease-fire, Sinn Féin was not allowed to participate until the cease-fire was restored in July 1997. At this point, refusing to negotiate with Sinn Féin, Ian Paisley's DUP and the UKUP abandoned the talks. This meant that a fringe portion of the Unionist community would not be represented from then on.

The distrustful relationships between the Nationalist and Unionist leaders meant that the negotiation process did not produce commitments on specific issues until the last week of the proceedings. Additionally, while the "nothing is agreed until everything is agreed" principle allowed the parties to negotiate more freely, it also allowed them to avoid committing to any concessions or proposals earlier in the negotiations. As SDLP delegate Sean Farren explained, "It was important that the Chair state that it was time to commit" (Farren 2014). In early 1998 Mitchell decided that "an early, hard deadline"

2. "Consultation Paper—Ground Rules for Substantive All-Party Negotiations" issued by the British government on Friday, March 15, 1996.

was necessary. However, it was not imposed but accepted by the parties "because they were eager as I was to get an agreement" (Mitchell 1999, 146). All agreed to meet continuously from March 30 to April 9 (Mitchell 1999, p.145). The Easter weekend deadline had symbolic value, as it was an important religious celebration for both communities, but more importantly, Mitchell wanted the referendum to be held in late May and for the new power-sharing assembly to be in place before the peak of the July parades, or *marching* season, which typically brought an upsurge of violence in Northern Ireland (Mitchell 1999, para. 145).

British Prime Minister Tony Blair and his Irish counterpart Taoiseach Bertie Ahern joined the talks in Belfast for the final and crucial week of negotiations. Disagreement over several issues threatened to derail the process during these last days of intensive negotiations. The independent authority given to the North-South bodies agreed upon by the governments on strand two arrangements was unacceptable to Trimble. More specifically, it triggered Unionist fears that it would become the precursor of a united Ireland, and required renegotiation. The early release of paramilitary prisoners was another divisive issue, with both Sinn Féin and the loyalist parties pushing for it, while the UUP resisted. Decommissioning remained a crucial issue as well. Despite the Mitchell Commission's recommendation, no arms were decommissioned during the negotiation process. The UUP insisted that a provision be included in the agreement, whereby decommissioning would be a requirement for participation in the new assembly. This was unacceptable to Sinn Féin and did not feature in the final agreement (Mitchell 1999, 171–81). After a forty-eight-hour-long complete lockdown during which none of the delegates was allowed to leave the Castle Buildings, the agreement was finally reached and signed on April 10, 1998, just one day after the previously set deadline.

On May 22, 1998, with a high 81.1 percent turnout, 71.1 percent of voters in Northern Ireland voted "yes" to the agreement. Although implementation was dependent only on an overall majority vote, as will be described in this chapter, it was important for the legitimacy and implementation of the agreement that it receive a majority of voter support in each of the communities. It accomplished this goal. However, while 96–97 percent of the Nationalist community voted "yes," the Unionist community was considerably less enthusiastic, with only 51–53 percent supporting the agreement.

Pressure and Confidentiality

George Mitchell's personal characteristics and his mediation skills are considered to have contributed to the success of the negotiations. All the party delegates I interviewed in Northern Ireland had an extremely positive view of Mitchell and his contribution to the peace process. Some emphasized his character, neutrality, and credibility (Maginness 2014), while others spoke of his personal skills and political experience (Empey 2014). In fact, Mitchell and his team's work were so highly appreciated that Jeffrey Donaldson, a UUP delegate in the negotiations (who joined the DUP thereafter), believed they should have continued to contribute well into the implementation process because "they were the ones who acquired the knowledge and understanding of the needs of both sides" (Donaldson 2014). Mitchell's facilitative and procedural mediation strategies were regarded as valuable to the process; he had the ability to listen and then sum up the parties' statements, "encapsulating all in a few words to allow us to move on," commented Alliance Party delegate Seamus Close (Close 2014). NIWC delegate Avila Kilmurray said this allowed the parties to focus on *what* was being said instead of *who* was saying it, and this helped them to find common ground (Kilmurray 2014).

Among the delegates, however, there was also a consensual perception that Mitchell was limited by the two governments during the last week of negotiations, when Blair and Ahern joined the talks. They had a general sense that the two governments hijacked the talks and that Mitchell, who had come to mediate upon their request, was sidelined. The governments requested that their proposal on strand two, giving independent authority to the North-South bodies, be put forward without changes and as a proposal issued by the mediation team. Mitchell knew this would be unacceptable to Trimble's UUP:

> To add to my already high anxiety, the government officials now requested on behalf of the prime ministers that we include in our comprehensive document what they had agreed on *without any changes.* They did not want a single word or a single comma altered. And we were told it should go in as *our* draft, not theirs. (Mitchell 1999, 160)

However, he and his team decided to respect the governments' request, understanding that part of their job as mediators was to "absorb blame" (Mitchell 1999, 156).

Although the British and Irish governments' participation was necessary (after all, the agreement required legislation from Dublin and Westminster) and generally regarded as positive, those in the UUP who did not support the agreement believed the British government's eagerness to put an end the paramilitary threat to Great Britain led it to push Unionists to concede more than they were ready to at the time (Empey 2014; Weir 2014).

Under pressure from Blair to accept the agreement as it stood on the last day of negotiations, Trimble put the agreement draft to a vote among all UUP delegates. As a small majority supported the agreement, the UUP endorsed the agreement. But some within the UUP thought the party was being forced to concede too much to Sinn Féin, particularly on the early release of republican (and loyalist) prisoners and the paramilitary decommissioning issues (Donaldson 2014; Weir 2014). The delegates who did not support the agreement left the building. This meant that just hours before the agreement was announced, the media reported on the UUP delegates abandoning the Castle Buildings. The internal divisions in the Ulster Unionist Party inevitably weakened the party's support for the agreement and its campaign. Some members of the party did not participate in the campaign and others were publicly vocal on their views against the agreement. The split in the Ulster Unionist Party then had a negative impact on the community's support for the GFA. Public opinion polls showed a rate of support for the agreement higher than 80 percent at the moment it was reached; this plummeted to 50–60 percent when Ulster Unionist leaders began to publicly express their reservations (Hayes and McAllister 2001, 78–80).

Secrecy was a significant feature of the peace process in Northern Ireland. The back-channel secret negotiations between the British government and the republican movement played a crucial role in forging communication and trust between the two actors, ultimately leading to the politicization and inclusion of Sinn Féin in the peace process (Dochartaigh 2011; O'Kane 2015). Although there has been interest in the study of secrecy in the broader peace process, this specific aspect of the All-Party Talks has not been analyzed.

With the exception of the "lock-down" during the last forty-eight hours of negotiations, the GFA negotiations were not held in *secret*. Winston Irvine, a delegate for the PUP, explained, "They were private, rather than secret" (Irvine 2014), and "confidentiality" was the term preferred by the majority of those I interviewed. Alban Maginness stated, "Confidentiality was important. I would not call it secrecy" (Maginness 2014). But confidentiality was valued by all; it was considered crucial for the parties to talk frankly and "to explore each other's positions," as Sinn Féin delegate Alex Maskey said (Maskey 2014). Even so, maintaining confidentiality was highly problematic during the negotiations. Information "leaks" were debated often and were a matter of concern to Mitchell, who feared they would lead to increased violence and disturb the negotiations by generating distrust and resentment (Mitchell 1999, 145).

Despite the desire for confidentiality, there was an overall understanding that the public should be informed about the negotiations to the fullest extent possible. For example, SDLP delegate Sean Farren perceived the negotiation process as relatively open because the parties were eager to give daily accounts to the media on progress (Farren 2014). The Alliance Party was keen to have the media aware of the negotiations because, as Alderdice explained, "We wanted, as far as possible, for the community to know what was going on and to feel positive about that" (Alderdice 2014). According to Alderdice, the Alliance Party felt that its agenda and preferences at the negotiations table were transparent and clearly known and supported by its constituency, hence their support of this type of engagement with the media.

The political leaders' willingness to speak to the media does not necessarily mean more information was available to the public on the negotiations. As Mark Devenport, a British Broadcasting Corporation (BBC) correspondent to the GFA negotiations, explained, political leaders tended to "spin" information to influence public opinion and "to influence the progress of negotiations inside the building" (Devenport 2014). However, the sheer number of participants in the talks favored journalistic access to information (Spencer 2010; Devenport 2014). The inclusion of more political parties meant the journalists had a larger pool and more diversified sources of information on what was happening at the talks—information they could pass on to the public.

The number of political parties participating in the All-Party Talks, therefore, significantly shaped the secrecy of the process. First, the large number made it difficult for the mediator to control outbound information to the media. Second, it allowed the inclusion of political parties more willing to have a less secretive negotiation process.

Political Inclusion

The politically inclusive GFA negotiations, as explained earlier, emerged from the wish of the British government to include the smaller Unionist parties associated with the loyalist paramilitaries. However, because Sinn Féin was absent initially and the DUP and UKUP later walked out, the All-Party Talks were never held between all ten elected parties at the same time. For this reason, the negotiations are often instead called the Multi-Party Talks.

Although multi-party, the negotiation dynamics were not multilateral. The talks did not unfold as a multilateral give-and-take process but rather relied on mediators shuttling between participants (Horowitz 2001a, 202; Alderdice 2014; Kilmurray 2014). In addition, while the process was inclusive, the GFA was mainly negotiated by the SDLP and the UUP. Horowitz (2002, 202, 218) sees this as a positive feature of the process because it allowed for a more coherent and implementable agreement to be reached. However, he does not consider the role that the bicommunal parties had in shaping the negotiation dynamics that brought about the agreement, nor their impact in bringing about an arguably implementable one. The Alliance Party's capacity to communicate with both Unionist and Nationalist parties helped build a good network of relationships at the negotiation table (Mitchell 1999, 44).

On the other hand, both the Alliance Party and the Women's Coalition had significant concerns about the implementation of the agreement and its long-term societal impact (Alderdice 2014; Kilmurray 2014). The inclusion of the Women's Coalition in particular meant that other issues beyond the distribution of power, which could be more easily agreed on, were brought to the negotiations table. For example, the Women's Coalition proposed the creation of a Civic Forum, which would function as a second chamber to the assembly and would operate through electoral colleges (i.e. the women's sector, the farmers' sector, the labor sector). They believed the forum to be particularly useful in dealing with more politically divisive issues during the implementation of the agreement by allowing civil society to discuss solutions without engaging in the stereotyped divisions of the political system (Kilmurray 2014). Unfortunately, the Civic Forum failed to fully materialize due the stagnating political period that came about with the implementation of the agreement.

Nonetheless, the political inclusiveness of the GFA negotiations is one of the merits of the process. Inclusivity brought in and strengthened the moderate parties' positions (Horowitz 2002, 218), and promoted the moderation of the more extreme parties' views. This allowed the agreement to be reached and favored its durability (McGarry and O'Leary 2006b, 262). Importantly, the inclusion of republican and loyalist paramilitaries reduced the possibility of the peace process being destabilized by paramilitary violence, which had sabotaged compromises in the past and polarized society (McGarry and O'Leary 2006b, 262). Because these groups, particularly republicans, were included and their claims legitimized, they had an incentive to adhere to the nonviolent, political pursuit of their claims (Toros 2008, 416–17). This has led some scholars to argue against labeling such groups as spoilers, since they might not necessarily be against peace, safeguarding that the preconditions for their inclusion must be clear to ensure their commitment to it (Cochrane 2008, 109; O'Kane 2010, 249–50).

Greater inclusion also meant that the varied political parties related differently to their constituencies; some were keener on informing their constituencies than others. For example, the Women's Coalition requested expert opinions on specific negotiation issues from the civil society groups and NGOs in its constituency. As NIWC delegate Avila Kilmurray explained, "The purpose was both to get expert views from the outside, but also to get buy-in for the [negotiations] process" (Kilmurray 2014). Other interviewees also described a close engagement with their constituencies, particularly the smaller paramilitary parties, like Sinn Féin and the PUP (Irvine 2014; Maskey 2014). Sinn Féin organized local area and town hall meetings where party leaders could filter and demystify information circulating in the media about the negotiation process:

> We would go to the social club and community center and invite people who were our supporters. They would be keen to know where things were at and what was happening at the moment, within the boundaries of the confidentiality or sensitivity . . . (Maskey 2014)

Because of their size, the smaller parties of Northern Ireland were typically more engaged with their constituents, keeping them informed during the negotiations and hoping to draw and keep their support.

The multi-party negotiation process also planted the seeds for wider political support for the agreement in the referendum; all the political parties who were signatories of the final agreement supported the "yes" vote, while those outside the negotiations, the DUP and the UKUP, made up the "no" campaign. The fact that the Nationalist community was fully represented in the negotiations and both the SDLP and Sinn

Féin supported the agreement meant Nationalist political support for the agreement in the referendum was comparatively higher than Unionist. As Alderdice explained,

> All the parties on the Nationalist side, all the parties in the Republic of Ireland, were supportive of it. On the Unionist side you had two political parties who were completely opposed to it—the UKUP, and more importantly the DUP—with very articulate leaders. (Alderdice 2014)

First, within unionism, there was a division in the referendum campaign period between the "yes" and "no" camps, and there was no such split in the Nationalist camp. The DUP, the UKUP, and a number of loyalist organizations—including the Loyalist Volunteer Force who broke with the Ulster Volunteer Force over the agreement—campaigned for the "no" vote (Irvine 2014). DUP leader Ian Paisley and UKUP leader Robert McCartney portrayed the GFA as a Unionist surrender to republican "terrorists." Their nationalistic and fear-inducing campaign messages played on the Unionist community's anxiety that the agreement would lead to a united Ireland (Somerville and Kirby 2012, 249). Second, while the PUP strongly campaigned for the "yes" (Irvine 2014), the split in the UUP during the final hours of the negotiations weakened its campaign. Members of the party were unwilling to participate in the "yes" campaign, and some were vocal in their opposition to the agreement. It must be noted that the DUP's self-exclusion from the negotiations allowed Trimble to be more accommodating, thus facilitating an agreement (Horowitz 2002, 218). However, it also meant political support was comparatively lower in the Unionist community and, more importantly, unlike the Nationalist community, it was targeted by a "no" campaign. Therefore, while the exclusion favored the arrival at an agreement, it had a negative impact on support in the referendum.

In sum, the political inclusivity of the GFA negotiations favored overall support for the agreement in the referendum. Although it was their own choice, the lesser inclusion of the Unionist political spectrum in the negotiations meant there was a discrepancy in Unionist and Nationalist political support for the agreement during the referendum campaign. This had a negative impact on the Unionist community's support—an impact I further explore later in this chapter.

Civil Society Inclusion and the Yes Campaign[3]

Northern Ireland had an active civil society that strove to be involved in the negotiations and pushed for the success of the peace process. Civil society organizations were spurred by the need to address issues of poverty and deprivation as political institutions were paralyzed by the conflict. With some exceptions, such as the Unionist Orange Order, the majority of civil society actors and organizations in Northern Ireland, whether in business, trade unions, churches, charities, or voluntary groups, were engaged in peacebuilding and reconciliation activities (Cochrane 2000; Kilmurray 2014). In fact, civil society's mobilization and its efforts to influence the negotiations were such that they helped sustain the momentum in the negotiations (Cochrane 2000, 2001), putting pressure on the political parties to reach an agreement (Alderdice 2014; Donaldson 2014; Farren 2014; Maginness 2014; Weir 2014).

Although the GFA negotiations included civil society, this was not the result of the desire or decision of the governments or the mediation team. Rather, civil society groups wanted to

3. Due to the need for differentiation, *Yes Campaign* refers specifically to the campaign led by civil society in Northern Ireland, while *"yes" campaign* is used to refer to either a specific or the overall campaign in support of the agreement.

be involved and have an influence on the negotiations. As a result of these groups' efforts, two forms of civil society inclusion took place in the GFA negotiations. The first, and most significant, was the direct participation of the NI Women's Coalition in the Multi-Party Talks. A more indirect form of inclusion took place through informal consultations that civil society representatives had with political party delegates. Although the Women's Coalition became a political party, it emerged from civil society and, as its delegates describe it, was a "civil society party" (Kilmurray 2014; Morrice 2014). The NIWC was formed in 1996 by a group of Catholic and Protestant women who saw the elections to the Peace Forum as an opportunity to have women represented at the talks. Because the electoral system was designed to favor the inclusion of smaller parties, it provided an opportunity for the women. The internal structure of the party was a coalition, not a traditional party, with two leaders—Monica McWilliams, a Catholic, and Pearl Sager, a Protestant—and its constituents included women from both denominations who were active in civil society.

Other civil society groups sought to influence the negotiations through informal consultations with political leaders. SDLP delegate Sean Farren said,

> Many organizations came to us to express their support and urge us to reach a settlement. Employers and trade unions combined. The main employer organizations, the Northern Ireland section of the Confederation of British Industries, and the main trade unions, all came to us to say they wanted us to succeed in the talks. (Farren 2014)

For example, the Northern Ireland Council for Voluntary Action (NICVA) worked as a platform to communicate information to its membership. "But that was informal. There was no formal organism to do that. We did it because we were aware of the importance of so doing," explained Quintin Oliver (2014).

Oliver became the director of the *Yes Campaign* led by civil society groups. Civil society's engagement with the negotiations continued through to the referendum, evolving into an active and successful "yes" campaign. A group of individuals and NGOs originally wanted to provide a platform for a unified, cross-community campaign, but they struggled to convince the political parties to join them (Oliver 2014). The UUP rejected the invitation due to its internal divisions. Empey, who coordinated the UUP's "yes" campaign, said the party did not accept the invitation to campaign under their umbrella because "[w]e had to get our own party to agree first, so our priorities were somewhat different . . ." (Empey 2014). Similarly, Alderdice (2014) argued that the parties had their own campaigns to run in the referendum and then for the assembly elections; he did not feel it was a realistic proposition to accept at the time. In the end, all parties, with the exception of the Women's Coalition (Bryan 2014), declined the invitation to join the platform and led their independent campaigns. As a result, the Yes Campaign worked independently from the political parties.

In the end, although the Yes Campaign was not the cross-party and cross-communal campaign it originally intended to be, Oliver believed this allowed it greater freedom than if the political parties had been involved (Oliver 2014). Over the six-week campaign period, the Yes Campaign strove to create positive debate around the referendum. Campaigning was done "partly by educating people" and providing "a framework for public digestion" of the agreement, as Oliver put it. The campaign used highly professional techniques, hiring the London-based advertising company Saatchi & Saatchi. It delivered a coherent message based on the benefits of the "yes" vote and the negative consequences of a "no" vote (Hancock

2011), at a time when the political parties' campaigns were using mutually exclusive arguments and some were delivering divisive messages.

In sum, the active role civil society played both within and outside the negotiations continued with efforts to mobilize support for the agreement in the referendum. As described, its long-term engagement in the peace process evolved into a resourceful and effective Yes Campaign.

Agreeing to Disagree

The *Agreement Reached in the Multi-Party Negotiations*, commonly known as the Good Friday Agreement or Belfast Agreement, provided for a power-sharing assembly with executive and legislative authority and institutionalized cooperation between the Northern Ireland and Irish executives and the British and Irish governments. The agreement provided for the safeguarding of human rights and equality, including the freedom of expression of religion and the freedom to pursue political aspirations, the right to equal socioeconomic opportunities in the communities, and the right to equal participation in politics for women.

Like the 1973 Sunningdale Agreement, the GFA acknowledged that the majority of people in Northern Ireland wished to preserve the union with Great Britain, but provided for a change in status if the majority consented to this change in a referendum. This allowed both Unionist and Nationalist political parties to claim that their right to self-determination was safeguarded. However, the agreement did not provide for concrete compromises on some of the most divisive issues. The reform of the Northern Ireland police—the predominantly Protestant Royal Ulster Constabulary (RUC)—and decommissioning were two of the most sensitive issues left to be resolved. Given the "nothing is agreed until everything is agreed" rule and the impossibility of an agreement being reached on these issues, the only possible compromise was that independent commissions would be established to decide, after the referendum, how they should be resolved (Morrice 2014). Essentially, the Northern Irish political parties "agreed to disagree" on some of the most difficult issues in the negotiations.

The "constructive ambiguity" of the agreement enabled political leaders to sign the agreement on April 10, 1998; importantly, it helped the political leaders "sell" the agreement to their constituencies in the referendum (Tonge and Evans 2002, 62; Dixon 2013, 114). However, in Aughey's view (2005, 147), while constructive ambiguity facilitated agreement, it harmed the implementation process by removing the need for important political commitments. This was problematic because it did not require more trustful relationships to develop between the parties[4]. Ambiguity was also problematic in the referendum.

Several elements of the agreement were particularly hard to sell for the UUP—especially prisoner releases and police reform. However, the agreement was "a very good outcome on the constitutional side" because "the Irish constitution changed" (Empey 2014). It was on the constitutional issue, namely that the agreement secured Northern Ireland's place in the United Kingdom, that the UUP's "sober" "yes" campaign looked to draw support from its constituency (Somerville and Kirby 2012, 245).

In contrast, the Nationalist political parties were fully in support of the "yes" vote, with the SDLP and Sinn Féin leading independent campaigns. Because the agreement would

4. The discussion of why the Good Friday Agreement faced implementation problems following the referendum is considerably more extensive. A significant debate centers on the electoral system forged by the agreement and whether it has contributed to segregation or integration in post-agreement Northern Ireland (Horowitz 2001b; Dixon 2005; McGarry and O'Leary 2006b).

bring about the political change desired by the Nationalist community, high support was expected; a "yes" vote guaranteed the Nationalist parties' and the Catholic community's access to the political establishment and allowed for Irish unity with the people's consent (Farren 2014; Maginness 2014). Additionally, holding the referendum in the Republic of Ireland at the same time the GFA referendum occurred in Northern Ireland allowed the Nationalist parties to frame the two referendums as an "all-Ireland" referendum; it was "the first time since 1918 that the Irish people as a whole could determine the shape of the island and make an agreement that would transform Irish politics," said SDLP delegate Alban Maginness (2014). The SDLP's "yes" campaign, nonetheless, had a conciliatory tone to draw the support of, or at least not alienate, voters in the Unionist community. The SDLP's campaign messages aimed to appeal to all in Northern Ireland by portraying the agreement as a win-win outcome and pointing to a new partnership and the reconciliation of the communities (Somerville and Kirby 2012, 242–44).

Despite the SDLP's conciliatory tone, the overall tone of the political parties' "yes" campaigns was divisive. On the one hand, the ambiguities of the agreement meant the campaign period was riddled with dissonant and sometimes zero-sum messages from the different "yes" campaigns. While Unionist political parties stressed the success of keeping Northern Ireland in the UK, Nationalist parties stressed the success of getting the principle of consent in the agreement. Also, by leaving issues to be decided by an independent commission, the agreement allowed Unionist leaders to claim decommissioning would take place after the referendum, while Sinn Féin claimed that no arms would be decommissioned before the establishment of the executive. Dixon (2013, 119–21) argues that Tony Blair played a part in "honorably deceiving" the Unionist community during the referendum campaign by publicly speaking about decommissioning provisions in ambiguous terms. Although constructive ambiguity favored political support for the agreement in the referendum, it allowed the UUP and Sinn Féin to use mutually exclusive messages in their campaigns that ultimately weakened the "yes" campaign overall (Somerville and Kirby 2012, 251–52).

Ulster Unionist leaders diminished the Unionist community's support for the agreement at the beginning of the campaign period, but Sinn Féin's campaign tactics amplified the negativity (Breadun 1998; Somerville and Kirby 2012, 246–47). Sinn Féin's campaign was framed as a "victory" and a step toward Irish unity. This had a negative impact on the Unionist community's support at a time when it was already divided (Clarke 2014; Irvine 2014). One particularly damaging publicity stunt was a "triumphant" welcoming of PIRA prisoners at a Sinn Féin special convention held just twelve days before the referendum. It was intended to bolster support within the republican community, where a fringe group did not support the agreement. However, since the early release of prisoners was one of the most controversial provisions of the agreement, the event had a negative impact on the Unionist community's public opinion (Breadun 1998). As PUP leader Winston Irvine described, "Republicans would come out saying that it was a victory for them and that they got everything that they need and the reaction to that from the other (Unionist) side was that 'we must be losing'" (Irvine 2014). Because support was dropping, Trimble accepted an offer to partner with the SDLP in attending a pop-rock concert given by the Irish band U2. On stage, John Hume and David Trimble publicly shook hands; the gesture worked as a symbol of unity strengthening the "yes" camp (Somerville and Kirby 2012, 247–48).

As for the information available to the public on the agreement, Northern Irish voters were generally knowledgeable about its content. There was public debate and extensive discussion in the media about its merits and shortcomings, but more importantly, a copy of the document was sent to every household in Northern Ireland by the British government. Beyond the ready access voters had to the document during the campaign period, the overall lines of the agreement were not new to the people in Northern Ireland. The agreements reached between the British and Irish governments in the decades before the GFA negotiations largely determined the overarching institutions set forth in it. Basically, the talks had focused on negotiating the details of how those overarching institutions would come to be. Therefore, the constitutional issues were part of public discussions as far back as the signing of the Sunningdale Agreement in 1973—so much so that Seamus Mallon, deputy leader of the SDLP during the GFA negotiations, described the GFA as the "Sunningdale for slow learners" (McLoughlin 2012). In addition, the local media largely supported the "yes" vote during the referendum campaign. In an unprecedented move, the *Irish News*, a Nationalist newspaper, and the *Belfast News Letter*, a Unionist newspaper, issued a joint editorial supporting the agreement (Graham 2014).

Although information on the agreement was readily available to voters, because the language of the document was ambiguous and some of the issues were left to be resolved by independent commissions, it was not possible for anyone to fully understand its implications. Liam Clarke, journalist for the *Belfast Telegraph*, explained, "The agreement was written in a way that you could not really have a detailed knowledge. It depended upon interpretation" (Clarke 2014). For this reason, Quintin Oliver from the civil society-led Yes Campaign believed that people looked for information, not by reading the content of the agreement, but by listening to politicians, businessmen, church leaders, artists, and other public figures whose opinion they trusted (Oliver 2014). Therefore, although the public was informed about the agreement, it was not necessarily the content of the GFA that shaped their vote.

Although the ambiguity of the agreement meant voters were potentially more influenced by political cues and the campaigns, this was not problematic for overall support because the majority of the political parties in Northern Ireland supported the "yes." In addition, the independent and strong civil society Yes Campaign targeted undecided moderate Unionists, the UUP's constituency, and helped raise support above the 50 percent threshold within this community (Hancock 2011). Nonetheless, the difference in support between the two communities reflected the winner-loser perceptions of the GFA process created during the referendum campaign. Lower support from the Unionist community would have likely undermined the legitimacy of the GFA's implementation and perhaps jeopardized the whole process.

An Inclusive Process with a Divided Outcome

The Good Friday Agreement negotiations brought to the table those involved in paramilitarism and transformed a violent conflict into, arguably, a solely political one. The process of the negotiation itself, the contact and communication between the leaders fostered by the process, significantly transformed political relationships (Alderdice 2014; Close 2014). As a result, life in Northern Ireland changed after the GFA. Paramilitary violence and fear are no longer an everyday experience.

The format of the negotiations, especially their inclusive character, contributed significantly to the high support the GFA received in the referendum. The political inclusiveness of the negotiations had a positive impact on reaching an agreement and, arguably, on implementing it (Horowitz 2002; McGarry and O'Leary 2006b). Inclusiveness also generated support for the agreement and ensured a positive outcome in the referendum. The fact that parties across the political spectrum participated in the negotiations and endorsed the final agreement meant that political support for the agreement was widespread.

The negotiation process was, however, comparatively less politically inclusive in the Unionist community than in the Nationalist community. The DUP and UKUP walkout and subsequent rejection of the agreement meant that the "no" campaign was only composed of Unionist political parties and targeted the Unionist community. In contrast, in the Nationalist community, both political parties, the SDLP and Sinn Féin, endorsed the agreement and supported and campaigned for the "yes" vote.

The inclusion of civil society also favored support for the agreement. Civil society's high engagement with the negotiation process and their push to be included evolved into a crucial role in the referendum. The strong, organized, and even professional Yes Campaign delivered unified campaign messages that were especially important in compensating for the UUP's lackluster campaign.

Although the GFA referendum had a positive outcome, the pressure on the UUP, together with the DUP and UKUP's "no" campaign, had negative repercussions on the Unionist community's support for the agreement. Tony Blair's pressure on Trimble to accept the agreement created a split in the UUP and weakened the party's support for the agreement. As Unionists composed the majoritarian community, and as the agreement would always mean sharing power with Nationalists, it seems logical that the Unionist community would always be less supportive. However, a majority was supportive of the process until the agreement was reached and the referendum campaign began. In addition, according to Hayes and McAllister (2001, 82–83), the "yes" vote in the Protestant community was influenced by a view of the agreement as "a new beginning."

This contradicts the intuitive idea that the Unionist community would be more averse to the agreement because it represented a change in the status quo, whereas change would be mostly welcomed by the Nationalist community.

Further, although the ambiguous text of the agreement allowed the political leaders to "sell" the agreement to their communities and constituencies, it also allowed them to campaign for the "yes" vote in different tones and using different arguments. These divisions during the campaign fostered perceptions in both communities that the Nationalists were the "winners" and the Unionists were the "losers" in the negotiations and the agreement. This, in turn, had an effect on the Unionist vote.

The inclusivity of the process also meant less secrecy in the talks. While some aspects of the final agreement were not known by the public—the early release of republican and loyalist prisoners, for example—people knew what an agreement would entail. Further, the text of the agreement was readily available to all in Northern Ireland. Previous agreements between the Irish and British governments, and even the early participation of the public in voting for who would take seats in the negotiations, allowed a generally unsurprising outcome—even though the fact that an agreement was reached at that point in time surprised many in Northern Ireland (BBC 1998).

Unfortunately, and despite its unquestionably positive outcome, the referendum experience and the split in the vote between the two communities, along with constant implementation setbacks, have generated a general sense in Northern Ireland that the agreement has not yet delivered on its promises and might collapse at any time, a fear that continues to polarize politics.

6

Comparing the Cypriot and Northern Irish Experiences

The Impact of Mediation Strategies

Past studies found that Álvaro de Soto's and George Mitchell's mediation strategies contributed to the "failure" of the Annan Plan initiative and the "success" of the GFA negotiations, respectively. However, these arguments tended to focus on why the agreement was reached by the political representatives, and not necessarily on why it was accepted or rejected in the referendum. In effect, *agreement reached* and *agreement accepted in a referendum* are two different outcomes that are not differentiated in most of the literature on the two case studies. Moreover, characteristics of the mediation process that experts believed to have led to the success of one case were absent from explanations of the failure of the other and vice versa. Since these assessments did not explain referendum results as effectively as they claimed to do, it remained, until now, to be explored whether and how mediation strategies affected the referendum experiences and outcomes.

As explained earlier in this book, some critics believe one of the (main) causes of the Annan Plan's failure was the secretive nature of the negotiations between political elites, with mediators failing to consider, involve, or gain support from other areas of society (Drath 2004, 341–52; Michael 2007;

Lordos 2009). If process secrecy could explain the rejection of the Annan Plan in the Greek Cypriot community, it remained to be explained why the Turkish Cypriot vote was not equally affected. In addition, if negotiation secrecy had shaped the Annan Plan referendum outcomes, it was important in this volume to ask if and how it affected the GFA referendum.

In the two cases, the degree to which negotiations were exposed to the public was a procedural characteristic of mediation with important consequences for the referendum. Comparatively, the GFA negotiations were less secretive. Interestingly, what made for a less secretive process in Northern Ireland was not a mediator's preference but rather an inadvertent consequence of the inclusivity of the process. The inclusion of more political parties meant that some of these parties were keener on informing their constituencies of the progress and content of the negotiations. The Alliance Party and the Women's Coalition both favored a less secretive type of negotiation, one that could help keep public pressure and sustain the momentum, or bring in civil society groups and their expertise on negotiation issues. The smaller paramilitary parties' closer engagement with their constituencies during the negotiations, alongside that of the Women's Coalition, also contributed to the lesser secrecy.

This more inclusive process also meant that journalists had a larger pool of diversified sources of information on what was happening *behind closed doors* than was the case in the Annan Plan negotiations. The Annan Plan negotiations were intentionally a more secretive process. In addition, since only the parties in power were represented at the negotiations, journalists had limited access to information. Consequently, Cypriots were generally uninformed, or disinformed, about the negotiations, in the Greek Cypriot community in particular. Secrecy predisposed the community to follow the cues of the stronger and highly politically backed "no" campaign for several reasons. It discouraged political leadership from confronting their constituencies and the general public about the issues and compromises under negotiation, which curtailed public debate and education at earlier stages of the process.

Studies on voting behaviors in referendums have shown that, when the issues at stake in the referendum are new or unfamiliar, voters tend to rely on information coming from the campaigns (Leduc 2002, 713). This has unique consequences for peace agreement referendums. If voters are uninformed and unfamiliar with the issues and compromises being negotiated, they will have to wait for the content of the agreement to be disclosed at the end of the negotiations and disseminated by the referendum campaigns. At the same time, the campaign periods will likely provide a short window of time for voters to understand the content of the agreement and digest some of its potentially difficult compromises. Further, the more voters look for, and wait for, information from the campaigns, the more volatile their voting decision-making will be. This will, on one hand, make the referendum result more unpredictable and, on the other, heighten the influence that the referendum campaigns will have on voters' decision-making. Consequently, secrecy can leave voters more vulnerable to "referendum spoilers" and "no" campaigns' fear-inducing messages, as the Greek Cypriot case best illustrates. This dynamic was counteracted in the Turkish Cypriot community because the community had greater engagement with the negotiations and public discussion of the Annan Plan before the referendum.

The two cases also show that, when agreements are not reached by the political leaders on their own terms, they have much less incentive to support them in a referendum. In Cyprus and Northern Ireland, pressure and arbitration reduced political accountability for the agreement, consequently affecting political parties' support and, hence, the shape and strength of the referendum campaigns. Arbitration reduced political support for the Annan Plan by allowing Papadopoulos and Denktash to deny accountability for the final agreement. As others have argued, the Annan Plan case shows that a peace agreement referendum is unlikely to succeed when the agreement is not endorsed by political leadership (Drath 2004; Kaymak 2012).

However, Papadopoulos's position on the Annan Plan did not only resonate with Greek Cypriot voters because the arbitration procedure allowed him to portray it as a bad agreement for his community; rather, the secrecy of the process and the consequent lack of voter information enabled Papadopoulos's framing of the agreement to reverberate within the community. The lack of communication to the public on the compromises needed to reach an agreement created false expectations of what would compose a compromise agreement. It left the community with a one-month referendum campaign to learn about and digest the agreement, and the "no" campaign gained momentum.

While secrecy predisposed the Greek Cypriot community to be more influenced by its leader, in the Turkish Cypriot community, Denktash's "no" campaign was counteracted by greater political and civil society support and mobilization for the "yes." As interviewees in the "yes" camp stated, the fact that Denktash's political opponents, civil society, and the media worked to stimulate public discussion about the Annan Plan helped dispel fears in the community about the aftermath of the referendum (Elcil 2014; Talat 2014).

In Northern Ireland, the British government's pressure on David Trimble to accept an agreement that did not provide a precise calendar for decommissioning split the UUP. The split weakened the party's "yes" campaign and helped divide voters in the Unionist community. In fact, political party splits had significant implications for both referendum experiences;

DISY and Serdar Denktash's DP are other two examples of how the decision to support an agreement can be internally divisive for political parties. Having to tend to their internal divisions, these political parties invested and mobilized fewer or no resources for their campaigns.

When a party split occurs, referendum studies have found that voters tend to lose confidence in the agreement (Schneider and Weitsman 1996, 604) and rely on information coming from the campaigns to make their voting decisions (Leduc 2002, 713). The implication for peace referendums here is that political party splits can make voters more dependent on the referendum campaign in deciding on how to vote and more prone to vote "no." Furthermore, when parties split over support for the agreement, their referendum campaigns are more focused on gathering or preserving political support from their constituencies, with an eye to future elections, and less on the referendum at hand. This opens up the referendum campaign period to competing campaign messages. This can damage voter support if it occurs on the "yes" side, as was the case in Northern Ireland. Similarly, the split in DISY was damaging to the "yes" campaign in southern Cyprus while, conversely, the split in Serdar Denktash's DP in northern Cyprus weakened the "no" campaign and therefore was not harmful to the "yes" vote in the Turkish Cypriot community.

One additional aspect worthy of comparison regarding the two mediations is the involvement "allowed" to the kin-states. The kin-states certainly played major roles in getting the political parties to agree in both Northern Ireland and Cyprus. Scholars are generally positive about the British and Irish governments' involvement in the negotiations in Northern Ireland (Byrne 2000; McGarry and O'Leary 2006a, 48). In Cyprus, the Turkish government is seen to have played a crucial role in making the Annan negotiations possible by pressuring and ultimately sidelining Denktash (Kocadal 2016). But others argue that the UN mediators in Cyprus incorrectly assumed the Greek government's support would enhance the support of Greek Cypriot political leaders and the Greek Cypriot community (Michael 2011, 185). Regardless of these nuances, when we consider the impact on the referendum campaign, their involvement is less benign. In Northern Ireland, the British government's "quasi-mediator" (Byrne 2000; Kocadal 2016) role and its pressure on the UUP reduced Unionist political support for the GFA in the referendum. Similarly, in Cyprus, Turkey's participation in the last round of negotiations, particularly Turkish Prime Minister Erdogan's speech to the media at Bürgenstock, fueled "no" campaign messages that Turkey had "won" the negotiations.

It can be difficult for a mediator to manage the involvement of kin-states. However, if kin-states are involved in the larger conflict, it is unlikely that peace negotiations will take place between the local communities' representatives without their support. In addition, their public support for the peace agreement garners support for the agreement in the referendum, as the case in the Turkish Cypriot and Nationalist communities. However, drawing from the two cases, less intrusive types of kin-state involvement in peace negotiations are potentially more desirable when agreements are ratified in a referendum. Taking Kocadal's (2016) typology, this means kin-states should act as *promoters*, not as *quasi-mediators*, *powerbrokers*, or *enforcers* in the negotiations, merely supporting or pressuring their "kin-community" to cooperate. Ideally, as authors who have studied the GFA negotiations suggest (Byrne 2000, 17; Kocadal 2016, 187), the kin-states should be able to cooperate with each other, as in Northern Ireland, although this is likely rare. More empirical research is needed on whether kin-states' involvement in negotiations or their leaders' public positions toward an agreement directly influence public perceptions of the agreement or referendum voting behaviors.

There are further implications for mediation theory and practice to be drawn from the comparison. First, procedural strategies have been found previously to have an insignificant impact on the outcome of a mediation process because they did not have a significant impact in getting the negotiating parties to an agreement (Bercovitch and Houston 2000, 175–76). However, both in Cyprus and Northern Ireland, the degree of secrecy under which the negotiations took place shaped the referendum outcomes. While the procedural aspects of the negotiations are unimportant when agreements are ratified solely by political elites, procedural decisions, such as the degree of secrecy under which the negotiations will take place, gain salience when the negotiations are followed by an agreement referendum. A certain degree of secrecy, or rather, confidentiality is crucial if political representatives are to discuss their positions and interests openly but, as others have argued, secrecy in peace negotiations has a cost (Wanis-St. John 2011). While mediators might find it beneficial to, for example, use secrecy to protect political leaders from the influence of less accommodating party members, they run the risk of alienating the public. This is especially important because political leaders are often the most important source of information for voters in referendums.

Second, and similarly, while directive mediation strategies are more effective in getting political leaders to reach a negotiated settlement (Bercovitch 1986; Bercovitch and Houston 1993, 2000), the two cases show that they may be counterproductive to that agreement being supported in a referendum. While pressure—a directive mediation tactic—may be effective in getting negotiating parties to an agreement, it can have a negative impact on support for the agreement in the referendum. Putting pressure on leaders and delegations to reach agreement can jeopardize a political party's support and weaken potential "yes" campaigns. If negotiators do not search for their constituents' support for the concessions they are making at the negotiations, pressuring leaders to accept an agreement can have negative repercussions on the peace agreement referendum further down the line. In fact, the need for tactics that generate artificial agreement on certain issues between political leaders in themselves signal unwillingness or inability to support or "sell" the agreement.

The analysis of the two cases shows that when a referendum is used to ratify a peace agreement, mediation strategies do, indeed, shape the referendum experience and outcome. Yet, the comparison has essentially highlighted that the strategies mediators use to facilitate agreement between the leaderships sitting at the negotiations table can affect whether or not that same agreement is supported in the referendum. In other words, the ways by which mediators promote leadership agreement may lead to the rejection of the agreement in the referendum. An agreement referendum, therefore, creates significant challenges for mediators in peace processes, which I return to in the next chapter.

Political Inclusion and Referendum Spoilers

Political inclusion is one of the most striking differences between the Annan Plan and GFA negotiations, the latter being decidedly more politically inclusive (not to be confused with multilateral). It is important to compare this aspect of the negotiations for several reasons. First, the inclusivity of the Good Friday Agreement negotiations has been time and again argued to have contributed to the "success" of the negotiation process (for example, Darby 2001; Curran and Sebenius 2003; McGarry and O'Leary 2006b), but an analysis of its impact on the referendum result was lacking. Second, research on referendums indicates that the public positioning of political leaders and parties on issues at stake in a referendum has often had the most significant impact on the campaign period and the referendum result (for example, Schneider and Weitsman 1996; Hobolt 2006; Vreese 2006). Therefore, it was important to understand if and how participation in the negotiations affected political leaders' or political parties' decisions to support, or not support, the agreement in the two cases. Thirdly, it was an aspect of the negotiations not previously studied in the Annan Plan case.

Ten political parties participated in the GFA negotiations, while the Annan Plan took place exclusively between the two Cypriot delegations. However, there was a comparatively greater inclusion of Turkish Cypriot political parties than there was for Greek Cypriot parties. As previously shown, Turkish Cypriot pro-solution opposition parties were informally included in the negotiations by the UN Good Offices Mission starting in 2002. While their original purpose was to put pressure on Denktash to negotiate, these parties had more substantial contact with UN mediators as Denktash began to lose popular support. After the 2003 elections, the Turkish Cypriot political moderates came to the negotiating table, later bolstering political support for the agreement in the referendum. The opposite was true for Greek Cypriots. When the "no" campaign gained momentum in the south, the political parties outside the negotiations struggled to maintain their support for the agreement. AKEL's switch to supporting the "no" vote, coupled with the split in DISY, meant that only a couple of political parties supported the agreement, while only a few politicians were actively involved in the "yes" campaign.

In sharp contrast, all the political parties who reached the GFA supported it in the referendum in Northern Ireland. By including a larger number of political parties, the negotiation process fostered political support for the agreement across the political spectrum. Exceptions were the DUP and the UKUP, who had abandoned the negotiations in the year before the agreement was reached. Political support for the agreement was, in effect, divided along the lines of who remained and who left the negotiations. It also meant that the Nationalist community was comparatively more politically represented in the negotiations—even fully represented—since both the SDLP and Sinn Féin remained in the talks, while a fringe of Unionist voters was then not. Additionally, while both the SDLP and Sinn Féin supported the "yes" vote, the self-exclusion of the two Unionist parties meant that the "no" campaign exclusively targeted Unionist voters.

The two cases show that the exclusion of political parties, even self-exclusion, has important repercussions on political support for the agreement and the strength of the referendum campaigns. This has implications for the debate on spoiler management. The negotiation process in Northern Ireland sidelined potential agreement spoilers and strengthened the more moderate positions and political parties by allowing the DUP and UKUP to leave of their own volition (Curran and Sebenius 2003, 150–51). This directly facilitated the remaining negotiators' ability to reach a peace agreement. However, their self-imposed exclusion removed any incentive for the two parties to support the agreement in the referendum, and, not surprisingly, they were against it. In the end, their "no" campaign helped divide support for the agreement in the Unionist community. Therefore, if removing "spoilers" can facilitate agreement at the negotiations table, exclusion creates incentives for these actors to oppose it in the referendum.

In Cyprus, sidelining Rauf Denktash, the main "spoiler," is considered one of the "successes" of the Annan mediation (Michael 2007, 598). Given his exclusion from the process, he unsurprisingly campaigned for the "no" vote. However, the greater inclusivity of the Turkish Cypriot political spectrum helped successfully manage Denktash as a referendum spoiler. Triggered by the political changes in the TRNC and Turkey, the more inclusive process and a more engaged community, especially in earlier stages of the negotiations, better prepared Turkish Cypriots for the referendum and diluted the impact of Denktash's support for the "no" vote. In the end, although both Cypriot leaders—Denktash in north Cyprus and Papadopoulos in the south—campaigned for the "no" in their communities, and did so using a similar rhetoric (Bryant 2004), the referendum outcomes were polar opposites.

The Annan Plan and the GFA show that politically inclusive negotiations help to create support for the peace agreement in the referendum. Wider political inclusion is desirable so that more political parties have political accountability and stakes in the agreement. This supports arguments in spoiler management literature that mediation processes should be (politically) inclusive (Darby 2001; Zahar 2003; McGarry and O'Leary 2006b). The more political parties are involved in negotiating an agreement, the greater the likelihood that those parties will endorse the agreement and, therefore, the wider political support. With more political parties supporting a "yes" vote, it is more likely that the campaign(s) for "yes" will be stronger.

Politically inclusive processes, however, present significant challenges to peace negotiations. A negotiation process that includes a greater number of groups with claims to political power runs the risk of causing further fragmentation at the table. The inclusion of armed groups, for example, is an enormous challenge to any peace process that requires clear rules for interaction and the effective promotion of their transformation into nonviolent actors (Dudouet 2010; O'Kane 2015; Planta and Dudouet 2015). However, in peace negotiations with agreement referendums, the agreement not only has to be reached but also has to be accepted in the referendum. As the two cases show, inclusivity is necessary to prevent the emergence of referendum spoilers and to manage the impact of their campaigns. In the end, even if an agreement is easier to reach with fewer negotiating parties, it can be rendered useless if it is rejected in the referendum. Therefore, when a referendum will take place to ratify the agreement, the advantages of including more actors may well offset those disadvantages.

Civil Society Inclusion and the Referendum Campaigns

There are compelling similarities in the two cases regarding the inclusion of civil society in the peace negotiations and its impact on the referendum. To begin with, both negotiations did not provide for any form of formal inclusion of civil society representatives. Where civil society inclusion took place, it was due to civil society groups' own efforts to influence the negotiations, rather than the result of a clear intent to include them. This was the case in Northern Ireland and in the Turkish Cypriot community, where civil society actively organized to create platforms that eventually allowed them to reach negotiators and mediators, or to have a seat at the table. In Northern Ireland, inclusion occurred through the Women's Coalition's direct participation and through other civil society groups' informal consultations with negotiation delegates. In Cyprus, Turkish Cypriot civil society pushed to be included and was able to have a limited influence on the negotiations and the agreement. This was achieved through the letter written to the UN secretary-general expressing Turkish Cypriot civil society's unified support for the negotiations, and the informal consultations that civil society leaders were able to have with UN mediators. Greek Cypriot civil society, on the other hand, did not significantly engage with the negotiations and no significant forms of inclusion took place there.

In both Northern Ireland and Cyprus, civil society actors were important referendum campaigners and their engagement with the negotiation process had a significant impact on the shape and strength of the "yes" campaigns. In Northern Ireland and in the Turkish Cypriot community, an engaged civil society was an important asset to the "yes" campaigns. In the Turkish Cypriot referendum, the unions and organizations who were part of the This Country Is Ours platform cooperated in leading the "yes" campaign. The involvement of Turkish Cypriot civil society groups from many areas, including business to education, and their cooperation with pro-solution parties elicited support for the negotiations across the community. In contrast, Greek Cypriot civil society only engaged with the Annan Plan process when the agreement was announced. It must be noted, however, that the "yes" campaign in the south was mainly led by civil society activists who took their own individual initiative. In the referendum, the few groups who campaigned for the "yes" were muffled by the rampant "no" campaign.

In the GFA referendum, like in the Turkish Cypriot community, civil society was highly engaged in campaigning for the "yes" vote. As described previously, the civil society–led Yes Campaign played a crucial role in the referendum. When we compare the two, however, Northern Ireland did not see the same level of cooperation of civil society groups and political parties during the campaign as in the Turkish Cypriot community in Cyprus. There was no umbrella "yes" campaign, and each of the Nationalist and Unionist political parties supporting the "yes" vote led their own independent campaigns. Regardless, the Yes Campaign was still crucial in providing a unified message of support for the agreement to encourage voters across the communal divide.

The similarities in the degree of engagement with the negotiations between civil society in Northern Ireland and in the Turkish Cypriot community are striking. In these two cases, the people, contacts, organizations, and platforms created and marshaled during the negotiations were then mobilized in the "yes" campaign. Although the forms of inclusion in the negotiations differed, we see a similar dynamic between the two, one that was absent in the Greek Cypriot community. Undoubtedly, some Northern Irish and Cypriot civil society groups did not support their respective peace agreements during the referendum. However, early mobilization potentially made civil society groups more effective campaigners for the "no" campaign, as demonstrated by the Pancyprian Citizens Movement in the Greek Cypriot community. Regardless, in the Annan Plan and GFA experiences, the civil societies that were more engaged in the negotiations were highly mobilised in the "yes" campaigns. This is evidence that including civil society groups in peace negotiations—inclusion being defined here in its broadest sense—encourages support for peace agreements in referendums.

These findings substantiate recent claims that the inclusion of civil society groups increases public support for the peace negotiation process (Barnes 2002; Belloni 2008; Nilsson 2012; Zanker 2014). Their campaigns can compensate for the hesitant support of political parties, which may be fearful of the political risk and cost of committing to an agreement that may be rejected in the referendum (Rao 2010, 10). In addition to this, including civil society in peace negotiations can stimulate groups to organize and mobilize at earlier stages of the peace process and encourage them to establish platforms for collaboration that can later be used to generate stronger "yes" campaigns in the referendum.

Agreement Design: Content versus Process Information

The Annan Plan and the Good Friday Agreement are two very different documents. The Annan Plan is an exhaustive document, with more than 192 pages (plus 250 pages of annexes) (United Nations 2003, para. 17). It was described by the secretary-general as "a truly comprehensive proposal, including all legal instruments necessary, and leaving nothing to be negotiated subsequently" (United Nations 2003, para.

61). The GFA is the polar opposite. Merely forty pages long, its text reflects the fact that the political parties of Northern Ireland "agreed to disagree" and left some of the most divisive issues to be addressed after the referendum.

When we compare the two cases to examine whether and how the contents of the agreement were relayed to voters, we see that the agreement itself was more readily available to voters in Northern Ireland than in Cyprus. In Northern Ireland, a copy of the final agreement was sent to every household; this was not the case in Cyprus, although smaller and more "readable" versions of the Annan Plan were distributed. The negotiation process in Northern Ireland also generally allowed greater public information on the issues under negotiation and the public had a sense of the general lines of agreement at an earlier stage of the negotiations. Greater information and public debate favored support for the agreement there.

Overall, the Nationalist and the Turkish Cypriot communities were comparatively more informed voters than their counterparts and both highly supported the agreements in their respective referendums. In fact, Hayes and McAllister (2001, 79, 82) found that, in Northern Ireland, "no" voters were less knowledgeable about the agreement than "yes" voters, with voters in the Nationalist community being the most knowledgeable. Greater public debate and access to information also potentially favored support for the agreement in northern Cyprus, where Turkish Cypriot voters were generally better informed about the Annan Plan than Greek Cypriot voters (Bryant 2004; Kaymak 2009), who were also misinformed and disinformed by political elites. The Nationalist and the Turkish Cypriot communities were both the minority communities in their respective cases and both naturally welcomed the new political realities the agreements would bring. While this may partially explain their support, it is also possible that these communities were more motivated for change because they were more engaged and better informed, which increased their support for the agreement.

It is important when seeking support to inform the community about the content of an agreement and its implications. However, this can be difficult to achieve. In Northern Ireland, the ambiguity of the text was problematic, while in Cyprus it was the length and legalistic language of the Annan Plan. For this reason, the negotiation process itself and the wider societal setting in which it takes place can play an important role in whether an agreement is supported or not in the referendum. While knowledge of the content of the agreement can influence voting behaviors, how the content is viewed in the overall context of the peace/reconciliation process is important for support. In this regard, the difference I found between the "yes" and "no" campaigners' views of the agreement both in Cyprus and Northern Ireland was telling: While Annan Plan and GFA supporters described it as a point in a process, or a way to move forward, those who campaigned for the "no" had more static views and described the agreement as an endpoint. Ali Erel, who supported the "yes" in the Turkish Cypriot community, said, "The agreement is just the start, the basis to work on and it is bound to have mistakes" (Erel 2014). Similarly, Marios Epaminondas, who campaigned for the "yes" in the Greek Cypriot community, stated, "This plan is good enough, it is not perfect but it is a way of moving forward" (Epaminondas 2014). In Northern Ireland, Empey described the GFA as a "work in progress to an extent" (Empey 2014), and Hayes and McAllister (2001, 82–83) found that "yes" voters tended to view the agreement as "a new beginning" while "no" supporters were more suspicious and believed they were the "losers" in the final agreement.

When we compare the cases to observe whether the agreement design shaped political support for the agreement, the conclusions are mixed. Agreement design was crucial to gaining political parties' support for the agreement in the referendum in Northern Ireland. Its ambiguities allowed political leaders to "sell" the agreement to their constituencies (Tonge and Evans 2002; Dixon 2013, 114) and, therefore, encouraged political support for the agreement in the referendum. The ambiguous agreement design allowed Sinn Féin to state that there would be no decommissioning prior to the establishment of the power-sharing government, while the UUP claimed that it would take place beforehand. It allowed for the Unionist political parties to campaign for an agreement that kept Northern Ireland in the UK, while republicans claimed to be a step closer to Irish unity. Yet it also allowed divisive views and disagreements to publicly persist between the leaders and, consequently, for antagonist interpretations of some of the provisions to coexist during the referendum campaign. While ambiguity can expedite the process of arriving at a satisfactory agreement between political leaders, it can negatively impact support in the referendum if those political leaders are unable to uphold less contrasting, zero-sum views.

On the other hand, the Greek Cypriot political parties' decision about whether to support the agreement or not suggests that the text of an agreement may not be the only, nor the most important, factor determining a political leader or party's support for an agreement in the referendum. Although Papadopoulos effectively "sold" the idea that the agreement was a bad outcome for Greek Cypriots, he did not negotiate with the intention of reaching an agreement that he would encourage his community to support. Equally, AKEL's support for the "no" vote and DISY's split support was not primarily due to dissatisfaction with the agreement, but mainly to tensions within the party.

As mentioned earlier in this book, an overall important implication that we can draw from the two cases is that caution is needed in reading an immediate link between referendum results and the contents of a peace agreement. This is partly due to an inadvertent wider tendency in the literature to assume symmetry between political leaders' positions and the people's voting behaviors. For example, Kaymak (2012, 89) argues that the Greek Cypriot veto of the Annan Plan signifies that "the Greek Cypriot voters would be keen to see substantively different elements embedded in any settlement package." While this opinion was voiced by Greek Cypriot political leadership, it does not necessarily reflect public opinion in the community. As has also been stated, other authors have argued that the Annan Plan did not sufficiently address the Greek Cypriot community's security concerns (Lordos 2009; Michael 2011, 186). However, if the people did not have a clear understanding of the contents of the agreement and were disinformed by their president about what a post–Annan Plan Cyprus would come to be, we cannot linearly interpret the referendum result as Greek Cypriot voters manifesting dissatisfaction with agreement provisions.

This is not to say, however, that what is agreed upon at the negotiation table is irrelevant in the referendum. The content of a peace agreement is crucial in accommodating political elites and creating implementable and durable post-conflict institutions. Also, the content of a peace agreement shapes public debates during a referendum campaign, even though that seems to have happened indirectly in the two case studies: in the way political leaders and the campaigns framed the agreement to their constituencies and how the media disseminated this information. The text of the agreement, nonetheless, appears to be a less important factor in shaping voters' decisions in the two cases, even though the questions asked in the referendum ballots referred precisely to it.

7

A New Paradigm in Peace Negotiations

What Process for the New Outcome?

The Annan Plan and GFA experiences show that an agreement reached by political leadership at the negotiation table and an agreement accepted by the people in a referendum are two very distinct outcomes. Moreover, the two cases provide evidence that a negotiation process that succeeds in bringing political representatives to an agreement may not work, and may even be counterproductive, to the agreement being supported in a referendum.

When there is a desire, a choice, or a requirement for a peace agreement to be ratified through a referendum, peace negotiations need to be adapted from the start. In this regard, a significant difference existed between the two negotiations—while the GFA negotiations in Northern Ireland took place with the knowledge that the agreement would be ratified by a popular referendum, this was not the case in Cyprus. The decision to hold a referendum came at a later stage in the Annan Plan negotiations and had the aim of bypassing the need for the political leaders' endorsement. While a more inclusive and private (rather than secret) process in Northern Ireland was both cause and consequence of the fact that the agreement reached would have to be accepted by the communities, the

Annan Plan negotiations were a traditional and exclusionary process that eventually culminated in a failed referendum.

First, mediators should be careful in the choice and mix of strategies they deploy. While isolating and putting pressure on political elites may be effective in bringing about agreements, secrecy prevents voter information and education, while pressure jeopardizes political support for the agreement in the referendum. Such processes reduce political accountability for the decisions that are negotiated and agreed upon. They further remove leaders' responsibility to inform and educate their constituencies and communities in a timely manner. Lack of voter education is consistently problematic in peace referendums, as was the case in the referendum in Guatemala in 1999, where the government failed to appropriately use resources to inform the mostly illiterate Mayan community about the agreement (Lee and Mac Ginty 2012, 64). Strategies that increase leaders' accountability for the peace process and favor public information are particularly important when an agreement referendum will take place at the negotiation's end. This necessitates a significant shift in the way peace negotiations have traditionally taken place.

Second, the more inclusive negotiations among the Turkish Cypriot political parties and in Northern Ireland indicate that including more political parties in the negotiations favors "yes" campaigns and fosters political support for a peace agreement. Conjointly, politically exclusive negotiations are more prone to create the conditions for effective referendum spoiling. This was also the case in the Colombian peace referendum in 2016, where the victory of the "no" vote surprised many at home and abroad after public opinion polls had indicated that the "yes" would win by a robust margin (Murphy and Cobb 2016). Defying all expectations, the peace agreement reached by the Colombian government and the FARC in Havana was rejected by a slight majority of voters, in a referendum with a low voter turnout. The agreement was negotiated exclusively between President Santos's delegation and that of FARC leader Rodrigo Londoño. It therefore excluded other parties, leaving Álvaro Uribe's Democratic Centre Party with an incentive to oppose the agreement and use the referendum for political gain (Tellez and Beardsley 2016). The rejection of the agreement then forced Santos to include the opposition in the renegotiations that started shortly after the referendum by bringing the Democratic Centre's proposals to the negotiations with the FARC. Instead of a new referendum, the new peace agreement was submitted for parliamentary ratification, where the agreement could not be rejected due to the government's majority. However, the Democratic Centre continued to gain politically from opposing the agreement in the referendum and, thereafter, came to power in 2018.

In fact, the importance of political inclusion to referendums in peace processes is gaining consensus in the literature. The meaning and form of this "inclusion," however, has been understood differently. Within the tradition of those who study consociationalism, particularly in Northern Ireland, the inclusivity of the institutions created and agreed to by the parties, and therefore enshrined in the peace agreement, has been found to be crucial to successful agreement referendums (Loizides 2015; McEvoy 2018). Institutional design is indeed critical to encouraging political elites to support the agreement; elites then typically have a significant influence on voter support in the referendum. However, while political elites and parties can significantly shape peace referendum results, we must keep in mind that it is not a given. Political support does not necessarily translate into support in the referendum.

A politically inclusive negotiation process will likely produce inclusive post-conflict institutional designs, as was the case in Northern Ireland. However, this is unlikely to be the case if the process is not inclusive. Inclusivity in the *outcome*—of the institutions enshrined in the agreement—will likely not take place without the antecedent political inclusivity of the *process*. For example, in the 2005 agreement referendum in Iraq, while Kurds and Shi'a Arabs overwhelmingly supported the new constitution in the referendum, the Sunni Arab community overwhelmingly rejected it. The lack of accommodation of the Sunni Arab constitutional preferences played a role in this rejection, which had considerable repercussions to the legitimacy of implementing the new constitution (McEvoy 2018, 873). Dissatisfaction with the agreement design among the Sunni Arab political elites had its inception in the marginalization of their representatives during the negotiation process (Morrow 2005). In Cyprus too, minority communities on the island, such as the Latin, Armenian, and Maronite communities, have largely been excluded from the negotiations throughout the years. Yet there is an opposing story to tell here. During the Annan Plan negotiations, after persistently reaching out to the Good Offices Mission and receiving a little help from the Vatican, Antonis Hajiroussos, the political representative of the Maronite community, was able to address the community's concerns regarding territory in the Annan Plan. A targeted campaign effort then followed to draw support from a community who was also being exposed to the rejectionist climate of the referendum campaign in the south. In the end, more than 90 percent of voters in the community supported the Annan Plan on the day of the referendum (Hajiroussos 2014).

Having many parties at the negotiations, with their competing interests and differing views on a solution, may be a greater challenge to reaching an agreement. However, the exclusion of political parties and groups who legitimately represent the interests of a community—or section of that community—can backfire when a referendum is used to ratify the agreement. Including more political parties or groups can prevent actors from later becoming referendum spoilers, as well as limit the impact of their "no" campaigns.

A third implication for peace negotiation and mediation that emerged from the comparison is that including civil society can potentiate support for the agreement in the referendum. Other studies found that civil society inclusion can *ripen* negotiations, increase grassroots support and political accountability, and bring about more durable agreements (Paffenholz, Kew, and Wanis-St. John 2006; Aljets, Chacko, and Jessop 2008; Nilsson 2012). As the Anna Plan and GFA experiences showed, when referendums are used to ratify peace agreements, civil society inclusion can foster public support for the agreement by contributing to the development of stronger "yes" campaigns.

Campaigns led by civil society groups can make up for less enthusiastic political party campaigns, or even serve as platforms that unite them. Elections for the new political institutions established in the agreement usually take place soon after the agreement referendum, which may reduce the political parties' incentive to invest resources in a referendum campaign. Moreover, political parties' "yes" campaigns can be divisive even if they are supporting the same outcome. For this reason, as the Annan Plan and GFA experiences also showed, unified campaign platforms and umbrella campaigns are desirable in peace agreement referendums. Civil society initiatives are uniquely suited to deliver such platforms and better able to provide a unified message of support for the peace agreement. In addition, civil society–led campaigns can shape the referendum campaign experiences significantly for the communities by promoting a discourse of compromise, tolerance, peace, and a common future. Free from electoral competition, their campaigns are better able to disseminate reconciliatory campaign messaging that helps to reduce polarization during the referendum campaign period.

In the event that a peace agreement referendum takes place again in Cyprus, there is cause for moderate optimism in this regard. Greek Cypriot civil society is more mobilized in support of a solution than it was during the Annan Plan negotiations. One symbolic example of this was the unprecedented joint support offered by the religious leaders of the two communities to the Anastasiades-Akinci negotiations (Andreou 2016a), which unfortunately failed at the very final stages in Crans-Montana, Switzerland, in June 2017. It is unlikely that the physical separation of the two communities will end before another referendum takes place, but cooperation between the "yes" campaigns on each side is possible. Civil society groups in each community could play a crucial role in delivering reconciliatory messages to the communities on both sides, but cooperation needs to take place much earlier and to a much greater extent than in 2004.

Including civil society can also balance confidentiality with the need for public awareness and participation (Wanis-St. John 2008), and mediators can create spaces that foster contact between civil society and political leaders during negotiations. As civil society actors are closer to the people, they are crucial information disseminators and can promote voter education. If civil society is included, the negotiations can be more transparent, and more information about the process will likely be available to voters at earlier stages of the negotiations. This is, however, not a given. Although in Colombia there was unprecedented concern for greater transparency and civic inclusion, perhaps due to optimistic but misguided expectations of the outcome, civil society did not sufficiently mobilize (ICG 2016, 11). Regardless, increasing transparency and civil society inclusion may advance changes in politically adversarial discourses and help to improve leaders' relationships during the negotiation processes; at the same time, transparency and inclusion may foster ownership and responsibility for the success of the peace process among both the leaders and the communities.

Fourth, the exploration of if and how the respective agreement designs shaped support in the two referendums brought into question whether the referendum results were actually a show of voter support or rejection of the content of the agreement itself. Because the agreement accommodates political interests, it is fundamental to have the support of political leaders and parties. For this reason alone, political support has a strong influence on the referendum outcome, since the opinions and positions of political leadership and parties are what tend to shape voters' decisions the most. Although the question asked in both referendums was whether voters accepted or rejected the peace agreements, the "yes" and "no" votes given by voters were not necessarily answers to the question. I return to the peace agreement referendum experience in Colombia. In October 2016, voters were asked whether they supported the agreement and the building of "a stable and lasting peace." Posing the question as such was, however, unsuccessful in preventing the majority of those who voted to "say no to peace." Although the "no" vote was victorious, we cannot infer that the people of Colombia, who have been through decades of conflict, do not want peace. In much the same way, we cannot reduce the result of a referendum to a clear answer to the question it posed and derive narrow political, or policy, implications from there.

Written agreements undeniably influence a referendum vote, if only because they deeply shape political support, the referendum campaigns, and the issues that are part of it. However, the timing of the information is crucial. It is especially for this reason that access to information about the negotiation process is important to gaining support for an agreement in a referendum. Voter education is essential to rebuff or counteract misinformation campaigns led by spoilers, such as those led by Papadopoulos and Denktash in Cyprus, or Paisley in Northern Ireland. However, a campaign period might be too short to allow voters to come to grips with agreements that are complex and whose implications are difficult, if not impossible, to grasp. Ignorance of the contents of the agreement was widespread in the areas most affected by the conflict in Colombia and contributed to the low turnout there (ICG 2016, 11). In addition, when voters are more dependent on the campaigns, political parties also have a greater incentive to invest in them, which generates greater competition between opposing campaigns. In a peace process, this competition can dangerously fuel polarization during the referendum. Because voter education cannot happen only during the campaign period, information about the negotiation process is crucial.

If the peace agreement will be put to a referendum, the negotiations must allow for public debate and engagement. This does not mean that negotiations should be completely open processes. Even so, as observed in the Turkish Cypriot and Northern Ireland cases, communication between political leaders, civil society groups, and the public during the negotiations is important to engage and educate the public at earlier stages of the process. Whereas the exclusive and secretive negotiation processes characteristic of peace negotiations have been geared toward getting political representatives or leaderships to an agreement, ratification by referendum calls for a radically different process.

To Hold or Not to Hold a Peace Referendum

Agreement referendums present significant challenges to peace processes. Because polarized referendum campaigns may reignite violence, scholars have debated whether referendums should be held at all. Moreover, peace negotiations are invariably such arduous and perilous processes and referendums are so highly unpredictable that holding a peace agreement referendum can understandably seem foolish. However, while failed peace agreement referendums may prompt the question of whether they should be held in the first place, they might not in themselves be the problem. The understanding that the Annan Plan and GFA peace negotiations shaped their referendum experiences and results, and the conditions and dynamics in which this happens, has significant implications for this debate.

Some scholars contend that, when it is politically feasible, referendums should not be used to ratify negotiated agreements (Loizides 2015, 142; Matanock and García-Sanches 2017, 153). "Silent elite pacts" are seen as a preferable alternative generally because the public will eventually support the agreement when the benefits emerge during implementation (Loizides 2015, 142). This argument was substantiated, for example, by the discovery of Bosnian support for the US-mediated Dayton Accords (Morgan-Jones, Loizides, and Stefanovic 2015). However, this requires that the implementation of an agreement leads to a relatively peaceful post-conflict situation, and this is not always the case. More often than not, agreements negotiated exclusively by political elites face implementation problems. The Oslo Accords reached between Israel and Palestine in 1993 failed to be implemented due to the exclusionist and secretive nature of the negotiations. The exclusionist process led to negative reactions to the agreement from those outside the negotiations, exacerbating spoiler problems and influencing public opinion. Wanis-St. John (2006, 141; 2011, 271–72, 286) argues that agreement implementation was undermined by the conditions of mistrust that created the need for secret negotiations in the first place. In the end, although placing a peace agreement to a popular vote can risk its rejection, an exclusive negotiation process can equally hamper its successful implementation.

South African–style mandate referendums may be an alternative option to a peace agreement referendum (Loizides

2015, 145–48), but in very specific circumstances. In a mandate referendum, a leader asks the community to support his or her efforts in reaching an agreement at the negotiation table. In this sense, mandate referendums can play a crucial role in allowing political leaders to balance democratic accountability with their legitimacy and credibility at the negotiation table. The elections to the Peace Forum in Northern Ireland functioned as a mandate-giving exercise (Cochrane 2000) and, indeed, favored public debate and engagement with the peace negotiations at an early stage of the negotiations. Like the elections to the Forum, mandate referendums can also work to familiarize the public with the content of the negotiations and bring the negotiation issues into public debate. In addition, they can also familiarize the public with the referendum process itself in societies where they are not common practice, which can be beneficial if there is also an agreement referendum further down the line.

However, holding a mandate referendum entails that the referendum will potentially be taking place at an early stage of the peace negotiations, and the peace process overall. This creates significant risks. Referendums in peace processes unavoidably deal with questions and issues with significant consequences for a society and are prone to heighten tensions and, in the worst case, to foster old and new polarization. For this reason, referendums that take place at an earlier stage of the peace process can lead to the resurgence of violence, as was the case in South Africa. While the South African referendum served to bolster those who supported the peace process, the opposite may be the case in other scenarios where those who oppose the peace process may gain ground, as Kaymac (2012, 107) fears would be the case in Cyprus. Nonetheless, the South African referendum was undeniably crucial to the peace process there and historically remarkable in marking the end of the apartheid regime. Yet the benefits that mandate referendums yield in fostering accountability and favoring legitimacy can potentially be achieved without the risks by less secretive and more inclusive peace negotiations.

An important debate that has taken place among those who study peace referendums is whether referendums can lead to violence re-escalation in conflict settings and, for that reason, are unsuitable for conflict resolution. Peace processes inherently have volatile contexts; therefore, the referendum experience runs the risk of stirring up conflict by further radicalizing public opinion (Mac Ginty 2003, 16–17). As in the Annan Plan and GFA "no" campaigns, campaign messages may rehash the very deep-rooted fears, insecurities, and hatreds that originally fueled the conflict (Reilly 2008, 233). Often referenced in this debate is the violence escalation after the results of the East Timorese independence referendum in 1999 were announced. Although it is true that the referendum experience can be problematic for conflict contexts, there is a growing understanding that referendums in themselves are not the source of the problem. Qvortrup (2014, 157) points out that violence in referendums is a rarity. In East Timor, he argues, violence was rather a consequence of the lack of clear agreement between parties on the legitimacy and ground rules for holding the referendum and the poor administration of the poll.

It is, in fact, increasingly consensual that referendums have specific requirements that need to be met in order to benefit peace processes (Lee and Mac Ginty 2012; Collin 2015, 2018; Loizides 2015). To avoid referendum failures and their negative consequences, the context must be prepared for the referendum experience. Prior conflict transformation work is desirable (Lee and Mac Ginty 2012; Collin 2018), not only to avoid having the referendum experience further polarize society and politics, but also to favor support for the agreement. Essential to this is that a conciliatory, win-win, or middle-ground discourse coexists with radical perspectives during the referendum campaign. But this needs to start during the negotiation process. Especially when peace agreement referendums are held, it is desirable that a certain degree of reconciliation has taken place during the negotiations so that the communities can say "yes" to an agreed future. Yet this is where peacemaking processes often fail by keeping the leaders' potentially accommodative behaviors out of the public eye and allowing radical views to linger in the communities. The victory of the "yes" in Northern Ireland marked a crucial turning point in the transition to peace. However, politics have remained polarized, and divisions between the two communities have lingered. The momentum created by the agreement and the mobilization of people during the referendum offered an opportunity for reconciliation that was not ideally harnessed. After the referendum, the decommissioning issue remained problematic. Win-lose perceptions of the agreement rooted in the campaign period were intensified by difficulties in the agreement's implementation. While the goal should be to have a majority vote "yes," as we have learned from Northern Ireland, the ideal is to have an agreement equally supported by the communities in conflict. However, for that to happen, it is necessary to have a certain degree of political reconciliation before the referendum.

Another concern raised about the use of peace agreement referendums is whether the public is actually apt to make decisions on the complex policy issues that referendums often address. However, the proposition that people are not well suited to make decisions regarding policies that can deeply affect their lives is a dangerous slippery slope. A referendum can only be a true instrument of direct democracy and expression of democratic will if it is exercised by well-informed voters (Schneider and Weitsman 1996; Hobolt 2007, 175–76). While voters have often been unprepared for referendums in the past, as was the case with the Greek Cypriot community, the important question is not whether the public is well suited for the referendum but rather why they have been unprepared and how this can be remedied in the future. Instead of deciding on whether voters are inept or not, our focus should remain on discovering how to potentiate voters' capacity to deal with and respond to the growing demands of healthy democratic processes.

As the Annan Plan and GFA experiences showed, the implication is that more transparent peace negotiation processes that engage with civil society and the public will promote greater voter education. This is especially important for peace agreement referendums because they invariably take place soon after an agreement is reached. Both in Cyprus and Northern Ireland, the referendums took place about a month after the agreements were reached or announced. While the date the Annan Plan referendum took place was purposefully set to, on the limit, take place before the EU accession agreement came in to force, agreement referendums typically happen soon after the agreement is reached in order to take advantage of the momentum created by its public announcement. The campaign periods alone are undoubtedly too short to allow for sufficient public education and debate (Lee and Mac Ginty 2012).

However, although longer campaign periods may result in better-informed voters, referendum campaigns tend not to be purely informational and can actually misinform voters. This has been problematic in other recent referendums. The "Leave" campaign in the 2016 EU membership—or "Brexit"—referendum in the United Kingdom admittedly misinformed and disinformed UK voters on the benefits of leaving the EU (Andreou 2016b). For UK citizens, and for the EU population at large, the European Union is an abstract and distant bureaucracy, often with institutions located "far away" in Brussels, and perceived to have little impact on the common EU citizen's lives. Although that is truly not the case, the ways in which being part of the EU has shaped EU citizens' lives is only accessible when one is informed and educated about what the EU is and how it works. Uninformed referendum voters are easy targets for opportunistic political leaders who may manipulate them and use the referendum to further their own political agendas (Schneider and Weitsman 1996, 584). Again, extending referendum campaign periods is not the solution. The potential "need" for a longer referendum campaign period signals that the public is unready for a referendum, possibly due to a lack of public and civic participation and/or secretive politics.

In peace processes, public education and debate can start at earlier stages and not exclusively during the referendum campaigns. As the Northern Irish and Turkish Cypriot experiences showed, greater inclusion of stakeholders and civil society is essential to reduce secrecy and promote public interest and engagement with the negotiations. Less secretive negotiations can push political leaders to seek support from those they represent for the positions and commitments they make, or do not make, at the negotiations table. This will potentially require politicians to educate their constituencies at earlier stages of the negotiations, allowing public debate to start sooner. Otherwise, the short time periods between the end of negotiations and the day of the referendum will likely be insufficient to educate voters not only on the text of the agreement but also, and perhaps more importantly, on how and why certain compromises were made. Unless there is a higher degree of political inclusion and an engaged civil society, whose concerns political leaderships hear, the small time periods between the end of negotiations and the day of the referendum does not suffice to educate the public.

All things considered, the significant challenges that holding referendums in peace processes present do not render them unsuitable for peacemaking. The unpredictability of a referendum result also does not imply that other forms of agreement ratification are preferable to an agreement referendum. No matter the arguments against them, the occurrence of referendums in peace processes is an increasing trend. They have become an important means of granting legitimacy to the political institutions devised in peace agreements (McEvoy 2018) and may well become the norm for agreement ratification. This means that peace referendums are probably here to stay, which might well render the question of whether or not they should take place irrelevant.

The ratification of peace agreements through referendums is rather not adequate for traditional types of peace negotiation processes. Peace negotiations that are exclusive and secret can marginalize and alienate the public. To use a form of direct democracy to decide on the implementation of an agreement is at odds with the traditional elitist and secretive way in which agreements have been negotiated. A referendum is a participatory tool that, for that very quality, demands a more transparent and participatory negotiation process. Peace agreement referendums require a negotiation process that can foster public interest and education; in addition, the process needs to be preceded by inclusive negotiations involving a broad spectrum of political stakeholders and creating opportunities for civil society inclusion and engagement with the wider public.

Conclusion

AGREEMENT REFERENDUM EXPERIENCES and results are affected significantly by the negotiation process that precedes them. Scholars have previously studied peace negotiations and their mediation to find out how they can lead to different sorts of agreements—from mere cease-fires to comprehensive settlements and their successful implementation—and less tangible outcomes such as the reduction of military tensions and the improvement of political relationships. Previous studies on peace negotiation did not consider how negotiations might shape referendum experiences and outcomes, while previous studies on peace referendums did not analyze how referendums are shaped by negotiation process conditions. Although certain features of negotiations were found to have shaped referendum experiences and results in peace processes around the world, a systematic and in-depth study of negotiations with the view of tracing their impact on referendums was lacking. The gap in academic research defied the reality that peace negotiations and the referendum experience are inseparable phenomena. After all, peace referendums ask voters about specific aspects, or outcomes, of the negotiations.

This book unravels the many important ways in which a negotiation process itself can affect whether an agreement is accepted or rejected in a referendum. The less secretive, more politically and civically inclusive process in Northern Ireland led to a higher level of political party support for the agreement and a stronger "yes" campaign, while the opposing dynamic was true in the rejection of the Annan Plan. In Cyprus, the secret and exclusionary negotiation process left Greek Cypriot voters vulnerable to the misinformation and cues provided by a politically backed "no" campaign, which led them to overwhelmingly reject the Annan Plan. The similarities between the negotiation and referendum experiences in Northern Ireland and among the Turkish Cypriot community were the most striking discovery. In both, the more inclusive character of the negotiation process generated support for the agreement in the referendum. Although the Annan Plan negotiations were formally more exclusionary than the GFA negotiations, the strong mobilization of opposition parties and civil society in support for the Annan Plan negotiations led to a more politically and civically inclusive negotiation process in the Turkish Cypriot community than was the case in the Greek Cypriot community.

What emerged from the study is that agreement referendums are not suitable for every kind of peacemaking process because a community's support for a peace agreement, regardless of its terms, cannot be gained overnight. When referendums are held to ratify a peace agreement, the process of their negotiation and mediation needs to be well thought out from the start. As a tool of democratic politics, peace agreement referendums must be preceded by inclusive negotiations involving a broad spectrum of political stakeholders and civil society, and must engage the public at early stages of the process.

Changes have begun to occur in peace negotiation and mediation practice in this regard with, for example, the growing involvement of civil society in negotiations. Involving civil society groups and engaging the wider public has been increasingly seen as crucial for the successful implementation of peace agreements and the establishment of enduring peace.

Although peace mediation has been studied—and indeed practiced—with a focus on the political elites, there is a growing recognition that peacemaking processes can no longer be solely a political affair. Although skepticism exists regarding the ability of peace negotiations to contribute to conflict transformation (Lederach 1997), we are only beginning to understand how they can more positively engage and include, and in this way shape, the societies and communities within which they take place. This book has contributed to this understanding by showing that the way peace negotiations are conducted can deeply shape the larger society's experience of the peace process, as they shaped the referendum experiences for the communities in Cyprus and Northern Ireland. It has highlighted the fact that peace referendums have a greater chance of succeeding if they are understood as a point in a process—a critical point in the reconciliation and transformation involved in the move from conflict to peace.

A great deal of research remains to be conducted on peace referendums, especially to analyze their role as an extension of the political process of peace negotiations. As I noted at the outset, studies based on public opinion polling can benefit from ascertaining what sources inform voter opinion, so that we can better understand *who*, *what*, *when*, and under what circumstances voters are informed and influenced. We also need to further probe the role of the media in peace process referendums. The media inform the communities and shape public opinion from the start of negotiations to the day of the referendum. In both Cyprus and Northern Ireland, the media were not neutral, merely aiming to inform the public and report the campaign. Rather, they favored the "yes" in Northern Ireland and northern Cyprus, and the "no" in the Republic of Cyprus. Regardless of their stance, the media were interested actors and, in both referendums, they played an important role in shaping public opinion.

Other types of negotiations with referendums can also benefit from more research. European treaties, bailout agreements, and other deals have been traditionally negotiated by European political elites behind closed doors. Examination of the level of secrecy/openness, political inclusion/exclusion, and engagement with civil society actors in different European institutions, and its impact on referendum outcomes could offer insights into whether transparent EU institutions could foster greater support for European integration.

As we expand and deepen the study of peace referendums, we can continue to build a theory, or theories, of what shapes peace referendums. The use of referendums for peace agreement ratification is a relatively recent phenomenon and work in this area is only beginning. Notwithstanding, this field of research is burgeoning as referendums are steadily taking place in peace processes around the world. They have become such a powerful legitimizing force, in fact, that it is increasingly common for a referendum to follow the announcement of a peace agreement. The emergence of peace referendums underscores the need for the democratization of peace negotiations and mediation and the need for further expansion on how they have been studied.

Referendums have become an undeniably important, and perhaps inescapable, peacemaking tool in contemporary peace processes. While we may rightfully acknowledge the high and diversified risks that holding a referendum in peace processes poses, the referendum experience itself can also positively shape the society in enduring ways and be a crucial positive step toward peace. Referendums are more than a one-off event; they are formative experiences in peace processes. Referendum campaign periods are sometimes the first opportunity for societies in conflict to experience and play out their political disagreements nonviolently. It is an opportunity for new visions and possibilities for the future to be publicly discussed and built.

A peace referendum can be an opportunity for the communities in conflict to come together in support of a common future, in spite of their disagreements on the details of that imagined future. Agreement referendums specifically can either aggravate divisions or help communities take a collaborative step forward, and the process of negotiating peace plays a fundamental role in shaping how they are experienced. As opposed to processes that end with agreements ratified exclusively by political elites, an agreement referendum requires less secretive and more inclusive and participatory negotiations that can help educate voters and prepare communities for the next stages of the peace process.

Bibliography

Index

Bibliography

Primary Sources

AKEL Politician. 2014. "Personal Interview by Author." Nicosia, February 27.

Akinci, Mustafa. 2014. "Personal Interview by Author." Nicosia, January 23.

Alderdice, John. 2014. "Personal Interview by Author." Belfast, June 28.

Andreou, Evie. 2016a. "Religious Leaders Pledge Support for Cyprus Talks." Cyprus Mail, February 10. http://cyprus-mail.com/2016/02/10/religious-leaders-pledge-support-for-cyprus-talks/.

———. 2016b. "Reality Check: Have Leave Campaigners Changed Their Tune?" *BBC News*, June 28. http://www.bbc.com/news/uk-politics-eu-referendum-36641390.

BBC (British Broadcasting Corporation). 1998. "Polls Show Pessimism in Peace Process," *BBC News*, March 5. http://news.bbc.co.uk/2/hi/uk/politics/62191.stm.

Breadun, Deaglan De. 1998. "Unionist Support for Agreement Drops Sharply, Poll Shows." *The Irish Times*, May 15. http://www.irishtimes.com/news/unionist-support-for-agreement-drops-sharply-poll-shows-1.152734.

Bryan, Dominic. 2014. "Personal Interview by Author." Belfast, June 19.

Clarke, Liam. 2014. "Telephone Interview by Author." Belfast, June 24.

Close, Seamus. 2014. "Personal Interview by Author." Belfast, June 24.

De Soto, Álvaro. 2004. "Letter from Álvaro de Soto to President Papadopoulos." April 23.

Demetriou, Panayiotis. 2014. "Personal Interview by Author." Nicosia, January 31.

Devenport, Mark. 2014. "Personal Interview by Author." Belfast, June 26.

Donaldson, Jeffrey. 2014. "Personal Interview by Author." Belfast, June 23.

Elcil, Sener. 2014. "Personal Interview by Author." Nicosia, January 21.

Empey, Reg. 2014. "Personal Interview by Author." Belfast, June 23.

Epaminondas, Marios. 2014. "Personal Interview by Author." Nicosia, January 29.

Erel, Ali. 2014. "Personal Interview by Author." Nicosia, February 14.

Farren, Sean. 2014. "Telephone Interview by Author." Belfast, June 30.

Faustmann, Hubert. 2014. "Personal Interview by Author." Nicosia, January 30.

Fokaides, Christoforos. 2014. "Personal Interview by Author." Nicosia, January 24.

Graham, William. 2014. "Personal Interview by Author." Belfast, June 5.

Hadjidemetriou, Takis. 2014. "Personal Interview by Author." Nicosia, February 25.

Hadjipavlou, Maria. 2014. "Personal Interview by Author." Nicosia, February 18.

Hajiroussos, Antonis. 2014. "Personal Interview by Author." Nicosia, February 13.

ICG (International Crisis Group). 2016. "Colombia's Final Steps to the End of War." Latin America Report N.58, September 7. https://www.crisisgroup.org/latin-america-caribbean/andes/colombia/colombia-s-final-steps-end-war.

Irvine, Winston. 2014. "Personal Interview by Author." Belfast, June 9.

Kentas, Giorgos. 2014. "Personal Interview by Author." Nicosia, January 17.

Kilmurray, Avila. 2014. "Personal Interview by Author." Belfast, June 27.

Kutay, Levent. 2014. "Personal Interview by Author." Nicosia, February 4.

Lillikas, Yiorgos. 2014. "Personal Interview by Author." Nicosia, February 24.

Maginness, Alban. 2014. "Personal Interview by Author." Belfast, June 25.

Maskey, Alex. 2014. "Personal Interview by Author." Belfast, July 2.

Morrice, Jane. 2014. "Personal Interview by Author." Belfast, June 30.

Murphy, Helen, and Julia Symmes Cobb. 2016. "Colombians Vote in Referendum on Peace Deal, 'Yes' Win Likely." *Reuters*, October 2. http://in.reuters.com/article/colombia-peace-idINKCN12204W.

Olgun, Ergün. 2014. "Personal Interview by Author." Nicosia, January 23.

Oliver, Quintin. 2014. "Personal Interview by Author." Belfast, June 19.

Özuslu, Sami. 2014. "Personal Interview by Author." Nicosia, February 3.

Papadopoulos, Tassos. 2004. "Letter from President Papadopoulos to Álvaro de Soto." April 20.

Papapetrou, Michalis. 2014. "Personal Interview by Author." Nicosia, February 5.

Pavlowitch, Kosta. 2014. "Personal Interview by Author." Nicosia, February 20.

Pericleous, Chrysostomos. 2014. "Personal Interview by Author." Nicosia, February 18.

Petasis, Aris. 2004. "Personal Interview by Author." Nicosia, January 24.

PIO (Press and Information Office of the Republic of Cyprus). 2004a. "2004: Mehmet Ali Talat, the New 'Prime Minister'—New York Meeting—Resumption of Talks in Nicosia and Burgenstock—G/Cs Reject Annan Plan—Republic of Cyprus Accedes to EU." http://www.moi.gov.cy/moi/pio/pio.nsf/All/90CF1FEB4B93B929C225783800399C01?OpenDocument.

———. 2004b. "Turkish Mass Media Bulletin 21.04.04." http://www.pio.gov.cy/moi/PIO/PIO.nsf/All/B9CC8224453B19A6C2256E7D003A991E?OpenDocument&print.

Potier, Tim. 2014. "Personal Interview by Author." Nicosia, January 20.

Talat, Mehmet Ali. 2014. "Personal Interview by Author." Nicosia, February 4.

Tzionis, Tassos. 2014. "Personal Interview by Author." Nicosia, February 25.

United Nations. n.d. "Civil Society." http://www.un.org/en/sections/resources/civil-society/index.html.

———. 2001. "Letter Dated 10 December 2001 from the Secretary-General Addressed to the President of the Security Council." S/2001/1162. http://kypros.org/UN/sg10dec.htm.

———. 2003. "Report of the Secretary-General on His Mission of Good Offices in Cyprus." S/2003/398. http://www.securitycouncilreport.org/atf/cf/%7B65BFCF9B-6D27–4E9C-8CD3-CF6E4FF96FF9%7D/Cyprus%20S2003398.pdf.

———. 2004. "Report of the Secretary-General on His Mission of Good Offices in Cyprus." S/2004/437. http://www.securitycouncilreport.org/atf/cf/%7B65BFCF9B-6D27–4E9C-8CD3-CF6E4FF96FF9%7D/Cyprus%20S2004437.pdf.

Vassiliou, George. 2014. "Personal Interview by Author." Nicosia, February 19.

Weir, Peter. 2014. "Personal Interview by Author." Belfast, June 16.

World Bank. n.d. "Civil Society: Defining Civil Society." http://web.worldbank.org/WBSITE/EXTERNAL/TOPICS/CSO/0,,contentMDK:20101499~menuPK:244752~pagePK:220503~piPK:220476~theSitePK:228717,00.html.

Secondary Sources

Adams, Gerry. 1997. *An Irish Voice: The Quest for Peace.* Kerry, Ireland: Mount Eagle Publications.

Alexiou, Alexis, Ayla Gürel, Mete Hatay, and Yiouli Taki. 2003. *The Annan Plan for Cyprus: A Citizen's Guide.* Oslo: PRIO.

Aljets, Diana, Betsie Chacko, and Maria Jessop. 2008. "The Ripe Moment for Civil Society." *International Negotiation* 13, no. 1: 93–109. doi:10.1163/138234008X297977.

Anastasiou, Harry. 2008. *The Broken Olive Branch: Nationalism, Ethnic Conflict, and the Quest for Peace in Cyprus, Volume Two: Nationalism Versus Europeanization.* Syracuse, NY: Syracuse Univ. Press.

Andersen, Pelle, Justin Bumgardner, J. Michael Greig, and Paul F. Diehl. 2001. "Turning down the Heat: Influcnces on Conflict Management in Enduring Rivalries." *International Interactions* 27, no. 3: 239–74. doi:10.1080/03050620108434985.

Anderson, Perry. 2008. "The Divisions of Cyprus." *London Review of Books* 30, no. 8: 7–16.

Aughey, Arthur. 2005. *The Politics of Northern Ireland: Beyond the Belfast Agreement.* New York: Routledge.

Bahcheli, Tozun. 2004. "Saying 'Yes' to EU Accession: Explaining the Turkish Cypriot Referendum Outcome." *The Cyprus Review* 16, no. 2: 55–66.

Barnes, Catherine. 2002. "Democratising Peacemaking Processes: Strategies and Dilemmas for Public Participation." *Conciliation Resources,* Accord Issue 13. http://www.c-r.org/accord/public-participation/democratising-peacemaking-processes-strategies-and dilemmas-public.

Barton, Brian. 2009. "The Historical Background to the Belfast Agreement." In *The Northern Ireland Question: The Peace Process and the Belfast Agreement,* edited by Brian Barton and Patrick Roche, 12–37. London: Palgrave Macmillan.

Baun, Michael, Jakub Durr, Dan Marek, and Pavel Saradin. 2006. "The Europeanization of Czech Politics: The Political Parties and the EU Referendum." *Journal of Common Market Studies* 44, no. 2: 249–80. doi:10.1111/j.1468-5965.2006.00622.x.

Beardsley, Kyle. 2011. *The Mediation Dilemma*. Ithaca, NY: Cornell Univ. Press.

Beardsley, Kyle, David M. Quinn, and Bidisha Biswas. 2006. "Mediation Style and Crisis Outcomes." *Journal of Conflict Resolution* 50, no. 1: 58–86. doi:10.1177/0022002705282862.

Bell, C., and C. O'Rourke. 2007. "The People's Peace? Peace Agreements, Civil Society, and Participatory Democracy." *International Political Science Review* 28, no. 3: 293–324. doi:10.1177/0192512107077094.

Belloni, Roberto. 2008. "Civil Society in War-to-Democracy Transitions." In *From War to Democracy: Dilemmas of Peacebuilding*, edited by Anna K. Jarstad and Timothy Sisk, 182–209. Cambridge: Cambridge Univ. Press.

———. 2009. "'Meditration' and 'Arbidiation' in Intractable Conflicts." *Ethnopolitics* 8, no. 2: 247–50. doi:10.1080/17449050902913050.

Bercovitch, Jacob. 1986. "International Mediation: A Study of the Incidence, Strategies and Conditions of Successful Outcomes." *Cooperation and Conflict* 21, no. 3: 155–68.

———. 2006. "Mediation Success or Failure: A Search for the Elusive Criteria." *Cardozo Journal of Conflict Resolution* 7: 601–15.

Bercovitch, Jacob, J. Theodore Anagnoson, and Donnette L. Wille. 1991. "Some Conceptual Issues and Empirical Trends in the Study of Successful Mediation in International Relations." *Journal of Peace Research* 28, no. 1: 7–17.

Bercovitch, Jacob, and Karl Derouen. 2004. "Mediation in Internationalized Ethnic Conflicts: Assessing the Determinants of a Successful Process." *Armed Forces & Society* 30, no. 1: 147–70. doi:10.1177/0095327X0403000202.

Bercovitch, Jacob, and Scott Sigmund Gartner. 2009. "New Approaches, Methods, and Findings in the Study of Mediation." In *International Conflict Mediation: New Approaches and Findings*, edited by Jacob Bercovitch and Scott S. Gartner, 1–15. New York: Routledge.

Bercovitch, Jacob, and Allison Houston. 1993. "Influence of Mediator Characteristics and Behavior on the Success of Mediation in International Relations." *Journal of Conflict Management* 4, no. 4: 297–321.

———. 2000. "Why Do They Do It Like This?: An Analysis of the Factors Influencing Mediation Behavior in International Conflicts." *Journal of Conflict Resolution* 44, no. 2: 170–202. doi: 10.1177/0022002700044002002.

Bew, Paul. 2007. *Ireland: The Politics of Enmity, 1789–2006*. New York: Oxford Univ. Press.

Biersack, John, and Shannon O'Lear. 2014. "The Geopolitics of Russia's Annexation of Crimea: Narratives, Identity, Silences, and Energy." *Eurasian Geography and Economics* 55, no. 3: 247–69. doi:10.1080/15387216.2014.985241.

Bryant, Rebecca. 2004. "An Ironic Result in Cyprus." Middle East Report Online, no. 12. http://www.merip.org/mero/mero051204?ip_login_no_cache=52fa9940f499cafcf6c89b45a06ddb89.

Burke-White, William W. 2014. "Crimea and the International Legal Order." *Survival* 56, no. 4: 65–80. doi:10.1080/00396338.2014.941548.

Burton, John. 1987. "Track Two: An Alternative to Power Politics." In *Conflict Resolution: Track Two Diplomacy*, edited by John W. McDonald and Diane Bendahmane, 65–72. Washington DC: Foreign Service Institute, US Dept. of State.

Byrne, Sean. 2000. "Power Politics as Usual in Cyprus and Northern Ireland: Divided Islands and the Roles of External Ethno-guarantors." *Nationalism and Ethnic Politics* 6, no. 1: 1–23. doi:10.1080/13537110008428585.

———. 2001. "Consociational and Civic Society Approaches to Peacebuilding in Northern Ireland." *Journal of Peace Research* 38, no. 3: 327–52. doi:10.1177/0022343301038003004.

Carment, David, Samy Yiagadeesen, and Souleima Achkar. 2009. "Protracted Conflict and Crisis Mediation." In *International Conflict Mediation: New Approaches and Findings*, edited by Jacob Bercovitch and Scott Sigmund Gartner, 216–39. New York: Routledge.

Cochrane, Feargal. 2000. "Beyond the Political Elites: A Comparative Analysis of the Roles and Impacts of Community-Based NGOs in Conflict Resolution Activity." *Civil Wars* 3, no. 2: 1–22. doi:10.1080/13698240008402436.

———. 2001. "Unsung Heroes or Muddle-Headed Peaceniks? A Profile and Assessment of NGO Conflict Resolution Activity in the Northern Ireland 'Peace Process.'" *Irish Studies in International Affairs* 12: 97–112.

———. 2006. "Two Cheers for the NGOs: Building Peace from below in Northern Ireland." In *A Farewell to Arms?: Beyond the Good Friday Agreement*, edited by Michael Cox, Adrian Guelke, and Fiona Stephen, 2nd ed., 253–67. Manchester Univ. Press.

———. 2008. *Ending Wars.* Cambridge: Polity Press.

Cochrane, Feargal, Bahar Baser, and Ashok Swain. 2009. "Home Thoughts from Abroad: Diasporas and Peace-Building in Northern Ireland and Sri Lanka." *Studies in Conflict & Terrorism* 32, no. 8: 681–704.

Collin, Katherine. 2015. "Do Referendums Resolve or Perpetuate Contention?" In *Contentious Elections: From Ballots to Barricades*, edited by Pippa Norris, Richard W. Frank, and Ferran Martínez i Coma, 111–30. New York and Oxon: Routledge.

———. 2018. "Peacemaking Referendums in Oceania: Making or Delaying Peace in New Caledonia and Bougainville." *Ethnopolitics*, September 13. doi:10.1080/17449057.2018.1513726.

Cotton, James. 2007. "Against the Grain: The East Timor Intervention." *Survival* 43, no. 1: 127–42.

Coufoudakis, Van, and Klearchos Kyriakides. 2004. *The Case against the Annan Plan.* London: Lobby for Cyprus.

Crocker, Chester A., Fen Osler Hampson, and Pamela R. Aall. 1999. *Herding Cats: Multiparty Mediation in a Complex World.* Washington DC: US Institute of Peace Press.

Curran, Daniel, and James Sebenius. 2003. "The Mediator as Coalition Builder: George Mitchell in Northern Ireland." *International Negotiation* 8, no. 1: 111–47. doi:10.1163/138234003769590686.

Curran, Daniel, James K. Sebenius, and Michael Watkins. 2004. "Two Paths to Peace: Contrasting George Mitchell in Northern Ireland with Richard Holbrooke in Bosnia-Herzegovina." *Negotiation Journal* 20, no. 4: 513–37. doi:10.1111/j.1571-9979.2004.00041.x.

Darby, John. 2001. *The Effects of Violence on Peace Processes.* Washington DC: United States Institute of Peace Press.

De Soto, Álvaro. 2002. "The Peacemaker: An Interview with UN Under-Secretary-General Álvaro de Soto." *The Fletcher Forum of World Affairs* 26, no. 1: 83–90.

———. 2012. "Can Cyprus Be Solved?" *Peace Review: A Journal of Social Justice* 24, no. 4: 398–405.

Dixon, Paul. 2005. "Why the Good Friday Agreement in Northern Ireland is Not Consociational." *The Political Quarterly* 76, no. 3: 357–67. doi:10.1111/j.1467-923X.2005.00694.x.

———. 2013. "An Honourable Deception? The Labour Government, the Good Friday Agreement and the Northern Ireland Peace Process." *British Politics* 8, no. 2: 108–37. doi:10.1057/bp.2012.30.

Dochartaigh, N. O. 2011. "Together in the Middle: Back-Channel Negotiation in the Irish Peace Process." *Journal of Peace Research* 48, no. 6: 767–80. doi:10.1177/0022343311417982.

Drath, Viola. 2004. "The Cyprus Referendum: An Island Divided by Mutual Distrust." *American Foreign Policy Interests* 26, no. 4: 341–52. doi:10.1080/10803920490502755.

Dudouet, Véronique. 2010. "Mediating Peace with Proscribed Armed Groups." Special Report No. 239, United States Institute of Peace, Washington, DC.

Durham, Helen. 2009. "From Paper to Practice: The Role of Treaty Ratification Post-Conflict." In *The Role of International Law in Rebuilding Societies after Conflict,* edited by Brett Bowden, Hilary Charlesworth, and Jeremy Farrall, 177–97. Cambridge: Cambridge Univ. Press.

Durkan, Mark. 1999. "The Negotiations in Practice." In *Accord: Striking a Balance: The Northern Ireland Peace Process,* edited by Clem McCartney, 36–43. London: Conciliation Resources.

Fearon, James D. 1994. "Domestic Political Audiences and the Escalation of International Disputes." *The American Political Science Review* 88, no. 3: 577–92.

Fitzduff, Mari. 2002. *Beyond Violence: Conflict Resolution Process in Northern Ireland.* New York: United Nations Univ. Press.

Franklin, Mark N. 2002. "Learning from the Danish Case: A Comment on Palle Svensson's Critique of the Franklin Thesis." *European Journal of Political Research* 41, no. 6: 751–57. doi:10.1111/1475-6765.00029.

Franklin, Mark N., Michael Marsh, and Lauren McLaren. 1994. "Uncorking the Bottle: Popular Opposition to European Unification in the Wake of Maastricht." *Journal of Common Market Studies* 32, no. 4: 455–72. doi:10.1111/j.1468-5965.1994.tb00509.x.

Franklin, Mark N., Cees van der Eijk, and Michael Marsh. 1995. "Referendum Outcomes and Trust in Government: Public Support for Europe in the Wake of Maastricht." *West European Politics* 18, no. 3: 101–17. doi:10.1080/01402389508425093.

Frazier, Derrick V., and William J. Dixon. 2006. "Third-Party Intermediaries and Negotiated Settlements, 1946–2000." *International Interactions* 32, no. 4: 385–408. doi:10.1080/03050620601011057.

Gartner, S. Sigmund, and Jacob Bercovitch. 2006. "Overcoming Obstacles to Peace: The Contribution of Mediation to Short-Lived Conflict Settlements." *International Studies Quarterly* 50, no. 4: 819–40. doi:10.1080/03050620601011057.

Georgiades, S. D. 2007. "Public Attitudes towards Peace: The Greek-Cypriot Position." *Journal of Peace Research* 44, no. 5: 573–86. doi:10.1177/0022343307080856.

Gilland, Karin. 2002. "Ireland's (First) Referendum on the Treaty of Nice." *Journal of Common Market Studies* 40, no. 3: 527–35. doi:10.1111/1468-5965.00368.

Greig, J. M. 2001. "Moments of Opportunity: Recognizing Conditions of Ripeness for International Mediation between Enduring Rivals." *Journal of Conflict Resolution* 45, no. 6: 691–718. doi:10.1177/0022002701045006001.

Greig, J. M., and Paul F. Diehl. 2006. "Softening Up: Making Conflicts More Amenable to Diplomacy." *International Interactions* 32, no. 4: 355–84. doi:10.1080/03050620601011032.

Haass, Richard N. 1991. "Ripeness, De-Escalation, and Arms Control: The Case of the INF." In *Timing the De-Escalation of International Conflicts*, edited by Louis Kriesberg and Stuart J. Thorson, 83–96. Syracuse, NY: Syracuse Univ. Press.

Hadjipavlou, Maria. 2002. "Developments in the Cyprus Conflict: A Conflict Resolution Perspective." Salzburg: Büro für Sicherheitspolitik.

Hancock, Landon E. 2001. "To Act or Wait: A Two-Stage View of Ripeness." *International Studies Perspectives* 2, no. 2: 195–205. doi:10.1111/1528-3577.00049.

———. 2011. "There Is No Alternative: Prospect Theory, the Yes Campaign and Selling the Good Friday Agreement." *Irish Political Studies* 26, no. 1: 95–116. doi:10.1080/07907184.2011.531107.

Handelman, Sapir. 2012. "Two Complementary Settings of Peace-Making Diplomacy: Political-Elite Diplomacy and Public Diplomacy." *Diplomacy & Statecraft* 23, no. 1: 162–78. doi:10.1080/09592296.2012.651970.

Hänggli, Regula, and Hanspeter Kriesi. 2010. "Political Framing Strategies and Their Impact on Media Framing in a Swiss Direct-Democratic Campaign." *Political Communication* 27, no. 2: 141–57. doi:10.1080/10584600903501484.

Hartzell, Caroline, and Matthew Hoddie. 2003. "Institutionalizing Peace: Power Sharing and Post-Civil War Conflict Management." *American Journal of Political Science* 47, no. 2: 318–32. doi:10.1111/1540-5907.00022.

Hartzell, Caroline, Matthew Hoddie, and Donald Rothchild. 2001. "Stabilizing the Peace after Civil War: An Investigation of Some Key Variables." *International Organization* 55, no. 1: 183–208. doi:10.1162/002081801551450.

Haskell, John. 2001. Direct Democracy Or Representative Government? Dispelling the Populist Myth. Oxford: Westview Press.

Hatay, Ann-Sofi Jakobsson. 2004. "Popular Referenda and Peace Processes: The Twin Referenda on the Annan Plan for a Reunited Cyprus Put in Perspective." *Daily News*, April 5. http://www.hurriyetdailynews.com/popular-referenda-and-peace-processes-the-twin-referenda-on-the-annan-plan-for-a-reunited-cyprus-put-in-perspective.aspx?pageID=438&n=popular-referenda-and-peace-processes-the-twin-referenda-on-the-annan-plan-for-a-reunited-cyprus-put-in-perspective-2004-05-04.

Hayes, Bernadette C., and Ian McAllister. 2001. "Who Voted for Peace? Public Support for the 1998 Northern Ireland Agreement." *Irish Political Studies* 16, no. 1: 73–93. doi:10.1080/07907180108406633.

Hennessey, Thomas. 1997. *A History of Northern Ireland 1920–1996*. London: Macmillan Press.

Herbolzheimer, Kristian. 2016. "Innovations in the Colombian Peace Process." *Conciliation Resources*, June. http://www.c-r.org/resources/innovations-colombian-peace-process.

Hobolt, Sara B. 2006. "How Parties Affect Vote Choice in European Integration Referendums." *Party Politics* 12, no. 5: 623–47. doi:10.1177/1354068806066791.

———. 2007. "Taking Cues on Europe? Voter Competence and Party Endorsements in Referendums on European Integration." *European Journal of Political Research* 46, no. 2: 151–82. doi:10.1111/j.1475-6765.2006.00688.x.

Horowitz, Donald L. 1985. *Ethnic Groups in Conflict*. London: Univ. of California Press.

———. 2001a. *Ethnic Groups in Conflict*, Updated Edition with a New Preface. Univ. of California Press.

———. 2001b. "The Northern Ireland Agreement: Clear Consociational, and Risky." In *Northern Ireland and the Divided World: Post-Agreement Northern Ireland in Comparative Perspective*, edited by John McGarry, 89–108. New York: Oxford Univ. Press.

———. 2002. "Explaining the Northern Ireland Agreement: The Sources of an Unlikely Constitutional Consensus." *British Journal of Political Science* 32, no. 2: 193–220. doi:10.1017/S000712340200008X.

Iklé, Fred Charles. 1964. *How Nations Negotiate*. New York: Kraus Reprint.

Interpeace. 2014. "An Innovation to Engage People in Peace Processes: Reflexions from Cyprus." Interpeace Report no. 2. http://3n589z370e602eata9wahfl4.wpengine.netdna-cdn.com/wp-content/uploads/2015/01/2015_01_06_PiP_Cyprus_Participatory_Polling.pdf.

Irwin, Colin. 1999. "The People's Peace Process: Northern Ireland and the Role of Public Opinion Polls in Political Negotiations." *Security Dialogue* 30, no. 3: 305–17.

Jarstad, Anna, and Desiree Nilsson. 2008. "From Words to Deeds: The Implementation of Power-Sharing Pacts in Peace Accords." *Conflict Management and Peace Science* 25, no. 3: 206–23. doi:10.1080/07388940802218945.

Johansson, P. 2009. "Putting Peace to the Vote: Displaced Persons and a Future Referendum on Nagorno-Karabakh." *Refugee Survey Quarterly* 28, no. 1: 122–39. doi:10.1093/rsq/hdp013.

Kaldor, Mary. 2000. "Introduction." In *Global Insecurity: Restructuring the Global Military Sector*, Volume III, 1–23. London: United Nations University.

Kaymak, Erol. 2009. "The Turkish Cypriot Views on Annan V." In *Reunifying Cyprus: The Annan Plan and Beyond*, edited by Andrekos Varnava and Hubert Faustmann, 143–58. New York: I.B. Tauris.

———. 2012. "If At First You Don't Succeed, Try, Try Again: (Re)Designing Referenda to Ratify a Peace Treaty in Cyprus." *Nationalism and Ethnic Politics* 18, no. 1: 88–112. doi:10.1080/13537113.2012.654078.

Ker-Lindsay, James. 2009. "The Emergence of 'Meditration' in International Peacemaking: A Response to Weller, Noel, Yakinthou and Belloni." *Ethnopolitics* 8, no. 2: 251–53. doi:10.1080/17449050902920204.

Kizilyürek, Niyazi. 2012. "The Turkish Cypriot Left. A Historical Overview." In *Beyond a Divided Cyprus: A State and Society in Transformation*, edited by Nicos Trimikliniotis and Umut Bozkurt, 170–84. New York: Palgrave Macmillan. doi:10.1057/9781137100801_10.

Kocadal, Özker. 2016. "A Conceptual Typology of Kin-State Mediation." *Negotiation Journal* 32, no. 3: 171–89. doi:10.1111/nejo.12158.

Kriesberg, L. 2001. "Mediation and the Transformation of the Israeli-Palestinian Conflict." *Journal of Peace Research* 38, no. 3: 373–92. doi:10.1177/0022343301038003006.

Kydd, Andrew. 2003. "Which Side Are You On? Bias, Credibility, and Mediation." *American Journal of Political Science* 47, no. 4: 597–611. doi:10.1111/1540-5907.00042.

Lederach, John Paul. 1997. *Building Peace: Sustainable Reconciliation in Divided Societies.* Washington DC: United States Institute of Peace Press.

Leduc, Lawrence. 2002. "Opinion Change and Voting Behaviour in Referendums." *European Journal of Political Research* 41, no. 6: 711–32. doi:10.1111/1475-6765.00027.

Lee, Joseph J. 1990. *Ireland, 1912–1985: Politics and Society.* Cambridge: Cambridge Univ. Press.

Lee, Sung Yong, and Roger Mac Ginty. 2012. "Context and Post-conflict Referendums." *Nationalism and Ethnic Politics* 18, no. 1: 43–64. doi:10.1080/13537113.2012.654085.

Loizides, Neophytos. 2009. "Pro: An Appraisal of the Functionality of Annan Plan V." In *Reunifying Cyprus: The Annan Plan and Beyond*, edited by Andrekos Varnava and Hubert Faustmann, 80–92. London and New York: Palgrave Macmillan.

———. 2014. "Negotiated Settlements and Peace Referendums." *European Journal of Political Research* 53, no. 2: 234–49. doi:10.1111/1475-6765.12043.

———. 2015. *Designing Peace: Cyprus and Institutional Innovations in Divided Societies.* Philadelphia: Univ. of Pennsylvania Press.

Lordos, Alexandros. 2004. "Can the Cyprus Problem Be Solved? Understanding the Greek Cypriot Response to the UN Peace Plan for Cyprus." Nicosia: Cyprus Market Research.

———. 2008. "Rational Agent or Unthinking Follower? A Survey-Based Profile Analysis of Greek Cypriot and Turkish Cypriot Referendum Voters." In *Cyprus: A Conflict at the Crossroads,* edited by Thomas Diez and Nathalie Tocci, 163–79. Manchester: Manchester Univ. Press.

———. 2009. "From Secret Diplomacy to Public Diplomacy: How the Annan Plan Referendum Failure Earned the Cypriot Public a Seat at the Negotiating Table." In *Reunifying Cyprus: The Annan Plan and Beyond*, edited by Andrekos Varnava and Hubert Faustmann, 163–79. New York: I.B. Tauris.

Lubbers, M. 2008. "Regarding the Dutch 'Nee' to the European Constitution: A Test of the Identity, Utilitarian and Political Approaches to Voting 'No.'" *European Union Politics* 9, no. 1: 59–86. doi:10.1177/1465116507085957.

Mac Ginty, Roger. 2003. "Constitutional Referendums and Ethnonational Conflict: The Case of Northern Ireland." *Nationalism and Ethnic Politics* 9, no. 2: 1–22. doi:10.1080/13537110412331301395.

Mandell, B. S., and B. W. Tomlin. 1991. "Mediation in the Development of Norms to Manage Conflict: Kissinger in the Middle East." *Journal of Peace Research* 28, no. 1: 43–55. doi:10.1177/0022343391028001006.

Maoz, Zeev, and Lesley G. Terris. 2006. "Credibility and Strategy in International Mediation." *International Interactions* 32, no. 4: 409–40. doi:10.1080/03050620601011073.

Matanock, Aila M. and Mihuel García-Sánches. 2017. "The Colombian Paradox: Peace Processes, Elite Divisions & Popular Plebiscites." *Deadalus, the Journal of the American Academy of Arts & Sciences* 146, no. 4: 153–66.

McEvoy, Joanne. 2018. "Letting 'The People(s)' Decide: Peace Referendums and Power-Sharing Settlements." *Democratization* 25, no. 5: 864–81. doi:10.1080/13510347.2018.1426568.

McGarry, John, and Brendan O'Leary. 2006a. "Consociational Theory, Northern Ireland's Conflict, and Its Agreement 2. What Critics of Consociation Can Learn from Northern Ireland." *Government and Opposition* 41, no. 2: 249–77.

———. 2006b. "Consociational Theory, Northern Ireland's Conflict, and Its Agreement. Part 2: What Consociationalists Can

Learn from Northern Ireland." *Government and Opposition* 41, no. 1: 43–63. doi:10.1111/j.1477-7053.2006.00170.x.

———. 2009. "Power Shared After the Death of Thousands." In *Consociational Theory: McGarry and O'Leary and the Northern Ireland Conflict*, edited by Rupert Taylor, 13–15. New York: Routledge.

McGrattan, Cillian. 2010. *Northern Ireland 1968–2008: The Politics of Entrenchement*. London: Palgrave Macmillan.

McKittrick, David, and David McVea. 2002. *Making Sense of the Troubles: The Story of the Conflict in Northern Ireland*. Chicago: New Amsterdam Books.

McLoughlin, P. J. 2012. *John Hume and the Revision of Irish Nationalism*. Manchester: Manchester Univ. Press.

Melaugh, Martin, and Fionnuala McKenna. 1998. "Results of the Referenda in Northern Ireland and Republic of Ireland." CAIN Conflict and Politics in Northern Ireland. http://cain.ulst.ac.uk/issues/politics/election/ref1998.htm.

Messiant, Christine. 2004. "Why Did Bicesse and Lusaka Fail? A Critical Analysis." *Conciliation Resources*, Accord Issue 15. http://www.c-r.org/print/book/export/html/1248.

Michael, Michális Stavrou. 2007. "The Cyprus Peace Talks: A Critical Appraisal." *Journal of Peace Research* 44, no. 5: 587–604. doi:10.1177/0022343307080857.

———. 2011. *Resolving the Cyprus Conflict: Negotiating History*. New York: Palgrave Macmillan.

Mitchell, George J. 1999. *Making Peace*. London: William Heinemann.

Moore, Gavin, Neophytos Loizides, Nukhet A. Sandal, and Alexandros Lordos. 2013. "Winning Peace Frames: Intra-Ethnic Outbidding in Northern Ireland and Cyprus." *West European Politics* 37, no. 1: 1–23. doi:10.1080/01402382.2013.801576.

Morgan-Jones, Edward, Neophytos Loizides, and Djordje Stefanovic. 2015. "Bosnians Would Vote for Dayton Two Decades On: Determining Support for Contested Peace Agreements." Paper Presented at the Conflict Research Society Conference, University of Kent, United Kingdom, September 14–16.

Morrow, Jonathan. 2005. "Iraq's Constitutional Process II: An Opportunity Lost." Special Report, December 1. United States Institute of Peace.

Moulakis, Athanasios. 2007. "Power-Sharing and Its Discontents: Dysfunctional Constitutional Arrangements and the Failure of the Annan Plan for a Reunified Cyprus." *Middle Eastern Studies* 43, no. 4: 531–56. doi:10.1080/00263200701348854.

Newman, Edward, and Oliver Richmond. 2006. "The Impact of Spoilers on Peace Processes and Peacebuilding." Policy Brief no. 2. Tokyo: United Nations Univ. Press. http://archive.unu.edu/publications/briefs/policy-briefs/2006/PB2-06.pdf.

Nilsson, Desirée. 2012. "Anchoring the Peace: Civil Society Actors in Peace Accords and Durable Peace." *International Interactions* 38, no. 2: 243–66. doi:10.1080/03050629.2012.659139.

O'Dowd, Niall. 2008. "The Awakening: Irish-America's Key Role in the Irish Peace Process." In *The Long Road to Peace in Northern Ireland*, 2nd ed., edited by Marianne Elliott, 67–77. Liverpool: Liverpool Univ. Press.

O'Kane, Eamonn. 2010. "Learning from Northern Ireland? The Uses and Abuses of the Irish 'Model.'" *British Journal of Politics & International Relations* 12, no. 2: 239–56. doi:10.1111/j.1467-856X.2009.00399.x.

———. 2015. "Talking to the Enemy? The Role of the Back-Channel in the Development of the Northern Ireland Peace Process." *Contemporary British History* 29, no. 3: 401–20. doi:10.1080/13619462.2014.987232.

O'Leary, Brendan, and John McGarry. 1993. *The Politics of Antagonism: Understanding Northern Ireland*. London: Athlone Press.

Paffenholz, Thania. 2014. "Civil Society and Peace Negotiations: Beyond the Inclusion-Exclusion Dichotomy." *Negotiation Journal* 30, no. 1: 69–91. doi:10.1111/nejo.12046.

Paffenholz, Thania, Darren Kew, and Anthony Wanis-St. John. 2006. "Civil Society and Peace Negotiations: Why, Whether and How They Could Be Involved." Oslo Forum 06 Background Paper. https://www.american.edu/sis/faculty/upload/Wanis-Civil-Society-and-Peace-Negotiations.pdf.

Papagianni, Katia. 2010. "Mediation, Political Engagement, and Peacebuilding." *Global Governance* 16, no. 2. Lynne Rienner Publishers: 243–63.

Pearson, Frederic S., Marie Olson Lounsbery, Scott Walker, and Sonja Mann. 2006. "Rethinking Models of Civil War Settlement." *International Interactions* 32, no. 2: 109–28. doi:10.1080/15325020600698728.

Pierce, Roy, Henry Valen, and Ola Listhaug. 1983. "Referendum Voting Behavior: The Norwegian and British Referenda on Membership in the European Community." *American Journal of Political Science* 27, no. 1: 43–63.

Planta, Katrin, and Véronique Dudouet. 2015. "Fit for Negotiation? Options and Risks in the Political Transformation of Non-Conventional Armed Groups." Norwegian Peacebuilding Research Centre Report, February. https://www.clingendael.nl/sites/default/files/Planta_Dodouet_NOREF_Fit%20for%20negotiation_Feb%202015_final_version.pdf.

Pruitt, D. G. 1997. "Ripeness Theory and the Oslo Talks." *International Negotiation* 2, no. 2. Brill: 237–50. doi:10.1163/15718069720847960.

Putnam, Robert D. 1988. "Diplomacy and Domestic Politics: The Logic of Two-Level Games." *International Organization* 42, no. 3: 427–60. doi:10.1017/S0020818300027697.

Quinn, David, Jonathan Wilkenfeld, Katheleen Smarik, Victor Asal, Kathleen Smarick, and Victor Asal. 2006. "Power Play: Mediation in Symmetric and Asymmetric International Crises." *International Interactions* 32, no. 4: 441–70. doi:10.1080/03050620601011107.

Quinn, J. Michael, T. David Mason, and Mehmet Gurses. 2007. "Sustaining the Peace: Determinants of Civil War Recurrence." *International Interactions* 33, no. 2: 167–93. doi:10.1080/03050620701277673.

Qvortrup, Matt. 2012. "The History of Ethno-National Referendums 1791–2011." *Nationalism and Ethnic Politics* 18, no. 1: 129–50. doi:10.1080/13537113.2012.654081.

———. 2014. *Referendums and Ethnic Conflict*. Philadelphia: Univ. of Pennsylvania Press.

Rao, Sumehd. 2010. "Citizen's Role in Political Settlements." Help-desk Research Report, GSDRC Applied Government Knowledge Services, Birmingham. http://www.gsdrc.org/docs/open/hdq1014.pdf.

Reilly, Ben. 2003. "Democratic Validation." In *Contemporary Peacemaking: Conflict, Peace Processes and Post-war Reconstruction*, edited by J. Darby and R. Mac Ginty, 1st edition, 174–83. London and New York: Palgrave Macmillan.

Richmond, Oliver. 1998. *Mediating in Cyprus: The Cypriot Communities and the United Nations*. London: Frank Cass Publishers.

Ron, Amit. 2009. "Peace Negotiations and Peace Talks: The Peace Process in the Public Sphere." *International Journal of Peace Studies* 14, no. 1: 1–16.

Ross, William H., and Donald E. Conlon. 2000. "Hybrid Forms of Third-Party Dispute Resolution: Theoretical Implications of Combining Mediation and Arbitration." *The Academy of Management Review* 25, no. 2: 416–27.

Ruane, Joseph, and Jennifer Todd. 1996. *The Dynamics of Conflict in Northern Ireland: Power, Conflict and Emancipation*. Cambridge: Cambridge Univ. Press.

Rubin, Jeffrey Z. 1981. *Dynamics of Third Party Intervention: Kissinger in the Middle East*. New York: Praeger.

Rubin, Jeffrey Z., and Bert R. Brown. 1975. *The Social Psychology of Bargaining and Negotiation*. New York: Academic Press.

Rynhold, Jonathan, and Asher Cohen. 2003. "Envisaging a Peace Referendum in Israel: The Legitimisation of Peace or a Legitimation Crisis? Lessons from Northern Ireland." *Civil Wars* 6, no. 1: 85–104. doi:10.1080/13698240308402527.

Savvides, Philippos K. 1998. "U.S. Foreign Policy toward Cyprus: Is the 'Theory of Continuity' Still Relevant?" *Journal of the Hellenic Diaspora* 24, no. 1: 31–59.

Schneider, G., and P. A. Weitsman. 1996. "The Punishment Trap: Integration Referendums as Popularity Contests." *Comparative*

Political Studies 28, no. 4: 582–607. doi:10.1177/001041409 6028004004.

Sciarini, Pascal, and Ola Listhaug. 1997. "Single Cases or a Unique Pair? The Swiss and Norwegian 'No' to Europe." *Journal of Common Market Studies* 35, no. 3: 407–38. doi:10.1111/1468 -5965.00068.

Scranton, Margaret E. 1993. "Consolidation after Imposition: Panama's 1992 Referendum." *Journal of Interamerican Studies and World Affairs* 35, no. 3: 65–102.

Sheehan, Edward R. F. 1976. "How Kissinger Did It: Step by Step in the Middle East." *Foreign Policy* no. 22: 3–70.

Smith, Daniel A., and Caroline Tolbert. 2009. *Educated by Initiative: The Effects of Direct Democracy on Citizens and Political Organizations in the American States.* 4th edition. Ann Arbor: Univ. of Michigan Press.

Solà-Martín, Andreu. 2007. "The Western Sahara Cul-de-Sac." *Mediterranean Politics* 12, no. 3: 399–405. doi:10.1080/1362 9390701622424.

Solsten, Eric. 1993. *Cyprus: A Country Study.* Washington, DC: Library of Congress.

Somerville, I., and S. Kirby. 2012. "Public Relations and the Northern Ireland Peace Process: Dissemination, Reconciliation and the 'Good Friday Agreement' Referendum Campaign." *Public Relations Inquiry* 1, no. 3: 231–55. doi:10.1177/2046147 X12448370.

Spencer, Graham. 2010. "Managing a Peace Process: An Interview with Jonathan Powell." *Irish Political Studies* 25, no. 3: 437–55. doi:10.1080/07907184.2010.497643.

Stedman, Stephen John. 1991. *Peacemaking in Civil War: International Mediation in Zimbabwe, 1974–1980.* Boulder, CO: L. Rienner Publishers.

———. 1997. "Spoiler Problems in Peace Processes." *International Security* 22, no. 2: 5–53. doi:10.2307/2539366.

———. 2001. "Implementing Peace Agreements in Civil Wars: Lessons and Recommendations for Policymakers." IPA Policy Paper Series on Peace Implementation, May, New York.

———. 2002. "Introduction." In *Ending Civil Wars: The Implementation of Peace Agreements*, edited by Stephen John Stedman, Donald Rothchild, and Elizabeth M. Cousens, 1–42. London: Lynne Rienner Publishers.

Stein, Janice Gross. 1985. "Structures, Strategies, and Tactics of Mediations Kissinger and Carter in the Middle East." *Negotiation Journal* 1, no. 4: 331–47. doi:10.1111/j.1571-9979.1985.tb00323.x.

Strauss, Annette. 1993. "The 1992 Referendum in South Africa." *The Journal of Modern African Studies* 31, no. 2: 339–60.

Svensson, Isak. 2007. "Mediation with Muscles or Minds? Exploring Power Mediators and Pure Mediators in Civil Wars." *International Negotiation* 12, no. 2: 229–48. doi:10.1163/138234007X223294.

Svensson, Palle. 2002. "Five Danish Referendums on the European Community and European Union: A Critical Assessment of the Franklin Thesis." *European Journal of Political Research* 41, no. 6: 733–50. doi:10.1111/1475-6765.00028.

Szczerbiak, Aleks. 2001. "Polish Public Opinion: Explaining Declining Support for EU Membership." *Journal of Common Market Studies* 39, no. 1: 105–22. doi:10.1111/1468-5965.00278.

Taki, Yiouli. 2009. "The Plan, Public Discourse and the Role of the Mass Media in Getting to 'No.'" In *Reunifying Cyprus: The Annan Plan and Beyond*, edited by Andrekos Varnava and Hubert Faustmann, 177–90. New York: Palgrave Macmillan.

Tannam, Etain. 2012. "The European Union and Conflict Resolution: Northern Ireland, Cyprus, and Bilateral Cooperation." *Government and Opposition* 17, no. 1: 19–73.

Tellez, Juan, and Kyle Beardsley. 2016. "Santos' Gambit and the Shadow of Domestic Politics in Peace Processes." *Political Violence at a Glance*, November 9. https://politicalviolenceataglance.org/2016/11/09/santos-gambit-and-the-shadow-of domestic-politics-in-peace-processes/.

Tonge, Jonathan, and Jocelyn Evans. 2002. "Party Members and the Good Friday Agreement in Northern Ireland." *Irish Political Studies* 17, no. 2: 59–73. doi:10.1080/714003201.

Toros, H. 2008. "'We Don't Negotiate with Terrorists!': Legitimacy and Complexity in Terrorist Conflicts." *Security Dialogue* 39, no. 4: 407–26. doi:10.1177/0967010608094035.

Touval, Saadia, and William Zartman. 1985. "Introduction: Mediation in Theory." In *International Mediation in Theory and Practice*, edited by Saadia Touval and I. William Zartman, 7–17. Boulder, CO: Westview Press.

Väyrynen, Raimo. 1991. "To Settle or to Transform? Perspectives on the Resolution of National and International Conflicts." In *New Directions in Conflict Theory: Conflict Resolution and Conflict Transformation*, edited by Raimo Väyrynen, 1–25. London: Sage Publications (CA).

Vreese, C. H. de. 2004. *Political Campaigning in Referendums: Framing the Referendum Issue*. New York: Routledge.

———. 2006. "Political Parties in Dire Straits?: Consequences of National Referendums for Political Parties." *Party Politics* 12, no. 5: 581–98. doi:10.1177/1354068806066787.

Wanis-St. John, Anthony. 2006. "Back-Channel Negotiation: International Bargaining in the Shadows." *Negotiation Journal* 22, no. 2: 119–44.

———. 2008. "Peace Processes, Secret Negotiations and Civil Society: Dynamics of Inclusion and Exclusion." *International Negotiation* 13, no. 1: 1–9.

———. 2011. *Back Channel Negotiation: Secrecy in the Middle East Peace Process*. Syracuse, NY: Syracuse Univ. Press.

Wanis-St. John, Anthony, and Darren Kew. 2008. "Civil Society and Peace Negotiations: Confronting Exclusion." *International Negotiation* 13, no. 1: 11–36. doi:10.1163/138234008X297896.

Wheeler, Nicholas J., and Tim Dunne. 2001. "East Timor and the New Humanitarian Interventionism." *International Affairs* 77, no. 4: 805–27. doi:10.1111/1468-2346.00220.

Yilmaz, Muzaffer Ercan, and Muzaffer Ercan. 2005. "The Cyprus Conflict and the Annan Plan: Why One More Failure?" *Ege Academic Review* 5, no. 1: 29–39.

Zahar, Marie-Joëlle. 2003. "Reframing the Spoiler Debate in Peace Processes." In *Contemporary Peacemaking: Conflict, Peace*

Processes and Post-war Reconstruction, 1st edition, 114–24. London and New York: Palgrave Macmillan.

Zanker, Franzisca. 2013. "Legitimate Representation in Mediation Processes: Civil Society Involvement in Liberia and Kenya." *Mediation Arguments* no. 1, Centre for Mediation in Africa, University of Pretoria, South Africa.

———. 2014. "Legitimate Representation: Civil Society Actors in Peace Negotiations Revisited." *International Negotiation* 19, no. 1: 62–88. doi:10.1163/15718069-12341270.

Index

accountability: arbitration and, 57, 75–76, 106–7; effects of civil society on, 25, 126; mandate referendums and, 7, 131–32; political elites and, 25, 114; political inclusion and, 114; public opinion and, 7, 123; secrecy and, 38, 76, 123

agreement design: content vs. process information, 117–21; political parties and, 17, 26–27; research design and, 43, 47; success vs. failure of, 17–18, 27, 37, 40–41, 124–25, 128–29; voters and, 8–9, 16–17

agreement referendum results, as negotiation outcomes, 6, 14–15, 21–22

Ahern, Bertie, 84, 86

AKEL (Progressive Party of the Working People), 53, 63–65, 112, 120

Akinci, Mustafa, 61–62, 65, 73, 127

Alderdice, John, 82, 88, 92, 95

Alliance Party, 81–82, 85, 88, 89–90, 105

All-Party Talks, 78, 82, 83, 87, 89, 100

Anastasiades-Akinci negotiations, 127

Anglo-Irish Agreement, 36, 78

Angola, 2, 2n1

Annan, Kofi, 35, 50, 53–55, 60, 67, 73

Annan Plan (Cyprus), 31–49, 50–77; background of, 35, 69–70; civil society mobilization and, 66–69, 76, 115–17; comparisons to GFA, 36–43, 104–21, 122–23; complexity of, 73–74; conditions of, 69–75; contextual factors affecting, 28; design of, 40–41; early stages of, 50–56; failure vs. success of, 7, 28, 37–41, 42, 51, 70–71, 75–77, 104–21, 113–14; legacy of, 122–36; mediation strategies, 36, 50–52, 57, 58, 104, 107, 110, 129; political inclusion and, 62–66, 105, 107–8, 111–15; referendum results and turnout, 37, 40, 42, 44, 56, 125; secrecy and, 37–38,

Annan Plan (Cyprus) (*cont.*) 56–62, 76, 77, 104–6, 107, 110; socioeconomic factors and, 29. *See also specific political party or organization*
arbitration: accountability and, 57, 75–76, 106–7; failure and, 37–38; as strategy, 44, 54–55, 56–62, 71–72
Aughey, Arthur, 97
Azerbaijan, 8

Balkan War, 35
Beardsley, Kyle, 20–21
Belfast Agreement. *See* Good Friday Agreement (GFA)
Belfast News Letter (newspaper), 100
Belfast Telegraph (newspaper), 100
Bercovitch, Jacob, 1–2
Bicesse agreement, 2
Blair, Tony, 84, 86–87, 98–99, 102
bombings, 33–34, 79
Bosnia, 130
Brexit, 134–35
British Broadcasting Cooperation (BBC), 88
British colonialism, 31

Canary Wharf, London, 79
cease-fires, 1–2, 32, 36, 79, 83
Christofias, Demetris, 53, 63–64
civil society inclusion: accountability and, 25, 126; importance of, 4–5, 7, 12, 18, 24–26, 37, 39–40, 115–17, 126–28; legitimacy and, 4–5, 24–25; mobilization of, 61–62, 66–69, 74–75, 76, 93–96, 101, 102; parameters of, 47; public participation as, 47; research design and, 43, 46–47; studies and surveys of, 126; sustainability of peace and, 4. *See also specific organization*
Clarke, Liam, 100
Clerides, Glafkos, 50, 64
Clinton administration, 36, 79
Close, Seamus, 82, 85
Cohen, Asher, 42
Colombia, 5, 6, 7, 123–24, 127, 128, 129
Communal Liberation Party (TKP), 61–62
communication facilitation: Annan Plan and, 107, 129; civil society and, 25, 40; GFA and, 101; as mediation strategy, 18, 19–20, 44–45; secrecy and, 87
confidentiality, 85–89, 110, 127
conflict management, 3–4, 5
conflict resolution, 3–4, 5, 6, 21, 132
Congo, 24
consociationalism, 26, 36, 124
Copenhagen European Council Summit, 52
credibility, 7, 76, 85, 131
Crimea, 8
crisis abatement, 20–21
CTP (Republican Turkish Party), 54, 55

CYBC (TV), 60
Cyprus: buffer zone, 32, 43, 54, 59; frozen conflict in, 43; origins of conflict in, 31–34, 59; post–Cold War, 35n1. *See also* Annan Plan (Cyprus); Greek Cypriots; Turkish Cypriots
Czech Republic, 8

Davenport, Mark, 88
Dayton Agreements, 35, 130
decolonization, 31, 59
Demetriou, Panayiotis, 72
Democratic Centre Party, 124
Democratic Party (DIKO), 53, 63–64, 65, 70, 71
Democratic Party (DP), 54, 65–66, 73, 108
Democratic Rally (DISY), 50, 52–53, 64–66, 68, 72, 108, 112, 120
Democratic Unionist Party (DUP), 39, 80, 83, 85, 89, 91–92, 102, 112–13
Denktash, Rauf: accountability and, 107; campaign rhetoric of, 61, 70, 114; Copenhagen Summit and, 52; misinformation campaign of, 128–29; sidelining of, 38, 39, 108–9, 113–14; strategies and tactics of, 50–62, 63, 65, 67, 71–73, 107, 112
Denktash, Serdar, 54, 65–66, 73, 108
Denmark, 13
De Soto, Álvaro: Akinci and, 65; civil society meetings with, 67; media climate and, 60; mediating role of, 35, 36, 45, 50; public support and, 73; strategies and tactics of, 50–51, 58, 104
directive (manipulative) strategies, 18–20, 21, 110–11, 135
Dixon, Paul, 98–99
Donaldson, Jeffrey, 85
Downing Street Declaration, 36
durability, 2–3, 20, 25, 90
Durham, Helen, 12, 22–23

East Timor, 6, 8–9, 132
Economic Community of West African States (ECOWAS), 24–25
EDEK (Movement for Social Democracy), 53, 63
EDI (United Democrats), 50, 64, 68, 71, 72
Egypt, 18–19
Elcil, Sener, 61
elites. *See* political elites
Empey, Reg, 95, 119
enduring rivalries, 3–4
enosis, 31, 32
Epaminondas, Marios, 58–59, 73, 119
Erdogan, Recep, 55, 76, 109
Erel, Ali, 67, 119
ethnonational conflicts, 8–9
European Community (EC), 34–35
European Constitution referendum, 28
Europeanization, 8

European Union (EU): Brexit, 134–35; Cypriot accession to, 29, 35, 38, 50–56, 77, 134; Czech Republic and, 8; growth of, 34–35; Ireland's accession to, 35–36; Netherlands and, 28; Norway and, 29; Poland and, 29; Switzerland and, 29; Turkey's accession to, 55, 70; United Kingdom's accession to, 35–36, 134–35
exit polls, 40

FARC (Revolutionary Armed Forces of Colombia), 6, 123–24
Farren, Sean, 83–84, 88, 94
formal agreements, 20–21
Forum, Peace (Northern Ireland Forum for Political Dialogue), 79–82, 94, 131
France, 13
Franklin's Theory, 12–13
FRELIMO (Mozambique Liberation Front), 25n2
full settlements, 18

Ginty, Mac, 9, 14, 17, 23, 28
Good Friday Agreement (GFA), 31–49, 78–103; ambiguity of, 96–101, 103; background of, 31–37, 78–85; civil society mobilization and, 93–96, 101, 102, 105, 115–17; comparisons to the Annan Plan, 36–43, 104–21, 122–23; decommissioning issue, 38, 79, 84, 87, 96, 99, 107–8, 120, 133; design of, 16–17, 40–41; implementation issues, 97n4; legacy of, 122–36; mediation strategies, 36, 38, 82–84, 85, 101, 104, 105, 110; negotiation principles, 82–84; political inclusion and, 89–93, 101–2, 105, 111–15; referendum results and turnout, 42, 44, 85, 87; secrecy and, 85–89, 105, 110; success of, 16–17, 37–41, 42, 70, 85, 93, 95, 98, 101–3, 104–21, 124. *See also specific political party or organization*
Greece, military junta in, 32
Greek Cypriots: buffer zone and, 32, 43, 54, 59; *enosis* and, 31, 32; EU accession and, 29, 35, 50–56, 77, 134; majority status of, 34; origins of conflict, 31–34, 59. *See also* Annan Plan (Cyprus); *specific political party or organization*
Guatemala, 7, 14, 17, 28, 29, 123

Haass, Richard N., 26–27
Hadjidemetriou, Takis, 71
Hadjipavlou, Maria, 59, 68
Hajiroussos, Antonis, 125
Hayes, Bernadette C., 102, 118
Holbrooke, Richard, 35, 52
Horowitz, Donald L., 89
Hume, John, 81, 99

inclusivity, 4–5, 23–26, 28, 39, 45–47, 124–25. *See also* civil society inclusion; political inclusion
Indigenous Rights Accords (Guatemala), 7, 14
Indonesia, 8–9
information. *See* public information
insecurity, 28
institutional design, 124–25
intangible outcomes, 1
International Body on Arms Decommissioning, 79
internet, role of, 11–12
Inter-Religious Council on Liberia, 25n1
Iraq, 7, 28, 125
Ireland, 31–34, 37, 79, 81, 82–83, 92, 98. *See also specific agreement; specific political party or organization*
Irish Nationalists: minority status of, 34, 102; origins of conflict in, 31–34. *See also* Good Friday Agreement (GFA); *specific political party or organization*
Irish News (newspaper), 100
Irish Republican Army (IRA), 33
Irish Unionists: majority status of, 34, 102; origins of conflict in, 31–34. *See also* Good Friday Agreement (GFA); *specific political party or organization*
Irvine, Winston, 87, 99
Israel, 18–19, 22, 130

journalism, 58–60, 74, 88–89, 100–101, 105

Kaymak, Erol, 121
Kenya, 24
Kilmurray, Avila, 85, 91
"kin-states," 45, 108–9
Kissinger, Henry, 18–19
Kocadal, Özker, 109
KTOS (Turkish Cypriot Teachers Union), 61
Kurds, 125

Leave Campaign, 134–35
Leduc, Lawrence, 13
Lee, Sung Yong, 14, 17, 23, 28
legitimacy: civil society inclusion and, 4–5, 24–25; mandate referendums and, 7, 131, 132; political inclusion and, 125–26, 136; secrecy and, 76; voter turnout and, 29, 42, 85, 101
leverage, as tactic, 18–19, 21
Liberia, 24–25
Liberian Bar Association, 25n1
Liberian Diaspora, 25n1
Liberians United for Reconciliation and Democracy (LURD), 25n1
Listhaug, Ola, 29
Loizides, Neophytos, 28–29
Londoño, Rodrigo, 124
Loyalist Volunteer Force, 92
LTDH (Tunisian Human Rights League), 25n3

Lubbers, M., 28
Lusaka agreement, 2

Maastricht Treaty, 13
Maginness, Alban, 87, 98
Mallon, Seamus, 100
mandate referendums, 7, 130–31
manipulative (directive) strategies, 18–20, 21, 110–11, 135
Mano River Women's Peace Network, 25n1
Markides, Alecos, 52
Marxist Popular Movement for Liberation of Angola (MPLA), 2n1
Maskey, Alex, 88
McAllister, Ian, 102, 118
McCartney, Robert, 80, 92
McGarry, John, 16–17, 46
McWilliams Monica, 94
media, 11–12, 74, 88–89, 121, 139. *See also* public information; *specific media*
media leaks, 36, 88–89
mediation strategies: impact of, 38, 39, 45, 50–51, 58, 85–86, 104–11; *pure vs. power* mediation, 20; research design and, 43, 44–45; studies on effectiveness of, 1–6, 18–20, 104; types of, 18–23, 44–45, 110, 123. *See also* arbitration; *specific strategy*
Michael, Michális Stavrou, 38
Middle East, post–Cold War importance, 35n1
Mitchell, George: appointments of, 79, 83; media leaks and, 88; personal characteristics of, 85–86; on procedural rules, 83–84; sidelining of, 86; strategies and tactics of, 38, 39, 45, 85–86, 104
Movement for Democracy in Liberia (MODEL), 25n1, 65
Movement for Social Democracy (EDEK), 53, 63
Mozambican National Resistance, 25n2
Mozambique Liberation Front (FRELIMO), 25n2
Multi-Party Talks, 78, 89, 94

Nagorno-Karabakh, 8
Nationalist parties. *See* specific *party*
National Unity Party (UBP), 50, 66
negotiation process conditions, 16–27, 28, 37, 41, 43, 48, 76–77, 137. *See also* agreement design; civil society inclusion; mediation strategies; political inclusion; spoiler management
Netherlands, 28
New Democracy Movement, 73
newspapers, 11, 74, 100
NGOs, mobilization of, 46, 68, 91, 95
Northern Ireland, origins of conflict in, 31–34. *See also specific agreement; specific political party or organization*
Northern Ireland Council for Voluntary Action (NICVA), 94–95

Northern Ireland Forum for Political Dialogue (Peace Forum), 79–82, 94, 131
Northern Ireland Women's Coalition (NIWC), 81–82, 85, 90, 91, 94, 95, 105, 115
Norway, 29

Olgun, Ergün, 73
O'Leary, Brendan, 16–17, 46
Oliver, Quintin, 95–96, 100
Orange Order, 93
Orthodox Church of Cyprus, 68
Oslo Accords, 22, 130
outcomes, 1–30; *agreement reached* vs. *agreement accepted*, 104, 122; definitions, 1–6, 7n2, 21–22; divided, 101–3; factors affecting, 9–15, 27–30, 39–41, 43–49, 110–11, 124–25; public information and, 12–14, 118, 123; tangible vs. intangible, 1, 19, 137. *See also* inclusivity; negotiation process conditions; *specific agreement*
Özuslu, Sami, 62, 74

Paffenholz, Thania, 46–47
Paisley, Ian, 80, 83, 92, 128–29
Palestine, 22, 130
Palestine Liberation Organization (PLO), 22
Panama, 8
Pancyprian Citizens Movement, 68–69
Papadopoulos, Tassos: accountability of, 57, 75–76, 106–7; campaign rhetoric of, 57, 59–61, 64, 70, 114; election of, 53, 63; EU accession and, 53–54, 77; misinformation campaign, 128–29; strategies and tactics of, 41, 55–56, 63, 70–73, 107, 120
partial settlements, 2
participatory mechanisms, role of, 4–5
Pavlowitch, Kosta, 60
peace agreement referendums, 1–30; campaigns for, 11–12, 29–30; definitions, 6, 48; political party support and, 10–11; pros and cons of, 129–36; studies and surveys of, 5–10, 14–15, 37, 137; timing of, 29; as a tool, 6–9; undemocratic aspects of, 8. *See also* outcomes; *specific agreement*
Peace and Democracy Party (PDM), 62
Peace Forum (Northern Ireland Forum for Political Dialogue), 79–82, 94, 131
peace negotiations, 1–30; challenges of, 8–9; characteristics of, 8–9, 18–27, 40–41, 43–49; contextual factors, 27–30, 132; future of, 122–36; influences on, 16–18; studies and surveys of, 1–6, 137; variables, 44–47. *See also* outcomes; *specific agreement*
peace studies, 1–6, 137
Petasis, Aris, 57
Poland, 29

political elites: accommodation of, 121; accountability and, 25, 114; implementation issues and, 130; institutional design and, 124; mediation strategy and, 123; power of, 4, 5, 6, 10–11, 13, 69; secrecy and, 104–5, 110, 123; "silent elite pacts," 130
political inclusion, 89–92; accountability and, 114; definitions, 45–47, 117; differences in, 62–66; European integration and, 140; importance of, 4–5, 18, 37, 101–2, 123–26; legitimacy and, 125–26, 136; public education and, 135; research design and, 43, 45–46; spoiler management and, 90–91, 106, 111–15
political parties: agreement design and, 17, 26–27; influence on voters, 12–14; kin-states and, 108–9; spoiler management and, 111–15; support and, 10–11, 43, 47–48. *See also specific party*
polls. *See* public opinion polls
Portugal, 2n1
power sharing, 3, 6–7, 26–27, 36, 78
procedural strategies: Annan Plan and, 36, 51–52, 57, 110; GFA and, 36, 38, 82–84, 85, 105, 110; as mediation strategy, 18, 19, 110; triple-lock system, 83
process conditions. *See* negotiation process conditions
Progressive Party of Working People (AKEL), 53, 63–65, 112, 120
Progressive Unionist Party (PUP), 80–81, 87, 91, 92, 99
Protestant Royal Ulster Constabulary (RUC), 33, 96
Provisional IRA (PIRA), 33, 34, 79–80, 83, 99
public diplomacy, role of, 4–6
public information: confidentiality vs., 88–89; Franklin's Theory, 12–13; lack of, 17, 22–23, 58–62, 74–75, 106–7, 135; outcomes and, 12–14, 118, 123; research design and, 43, 48–49; sources of, 10–11; studies and surveys of, 48–49
public opinion: accountability and, 7, 123; managing and shaping of, 5, 12, 88–89, 130, 139; "public" defined, 7n2; radicalization of, 9, 132; studies and surveys of, 14–15, 74–75, 139
public opinion polls, 5, 14–15, 40, 47, 64, 87, 123–24, 139
public participation, 47
pure vs. power mediation, 20
Putnam, Robert, 16

Qvortrup, Matt, 5, 132

radio, 11, 62, 74
referendum campaigns, 48. *See also* peace agreement referendums

Republican Turkish Party (CTP), 54, 65
Republic of Cyprus. *See* Cyprus
Republic of Ireland. *See* Ireland
Revolutionary Armed Forces of Colombia (FARC), 6, 123–24
Rome General Peace Accords, 25n2
RUC (Protestant Royal Ulster Constabulary), 33, 96
Russian Federation, 8
Rwanda, 2, 7, 28, 29
Rynhold, Jonathan, 42

Saatchi & Saatchi, 95–96
Sager, Pearl, 94
Santos, Juan Manuel, 124
Savimbi, Jonas, 2n1
Schneider, G., 13
Sciarini, Pascal, 29
Scranton, Margaret E., 7–8
secrecy, 56–62; accountability and, 38, 76, 123; confidentiality and, 85–89, 110, 127; inclusivity and, 103, 104–6, 140; lack of information and, 17, 22–23, 58–62, 74–75, 106–7, 135; legitimacy and, 76; political elites and, 104–5, 110, 123; studies and surveys of, 4, 22; as tactic, 21–23, 37–39, 77, 87–89, 110, 123, 140
self-determination, 6–7, 8, 96
Shi'a Arabs, 125
sidelining, 38, 39, 86, 108–9, 113–14
Sierra Leone, 2, 24
"Silent elite pacts," 130
SIM, 62
Sinn Féin: campaign tactics, 99; concessions to, 87; conditions of, 33, 81, 84, 88, 97–98, 99, 102, 120; PIRA and, 80n1; political inclusion and, 91–92, 113; stakeholder status and, 39, 83; United States and, 36
Social Democratic and Labour Party (SDLP): civil society inclusion and, 94; collapse of Parliament and, 34; confidentiality and, 88; Northern Ireland Forum for Political Dialogue and, 94; political inclusion and, 89, 91, 113; strategies and tactics of, 83–84, 97–98, 99, 100, 102
social media, role of, 11–12
socioeconomic conditions, 29
Somalia, 2
South Africa, 6–7, 130–32
South Sudan, 6, 29
Sovereign Base Areas, 69–70
spoiler management, 23–24, 39, 90–91, 106, 111–15, 126, 128–29, 130
Sri Lanka, 2
status quo, 23
Stedman, Stephen John, 23, 24, 26–27
Sunni Arabs, 125
Sunningdale Agreement, 36, 78, 96, 100
Svensson, Isak, 20
Switzerland, 29

Taki, Yiouli, 60
taksim, 31
Talat, Mehmet Ali, 54, 55, 61–62, 65–66, 72, 73
tangible outcomes, 1
television, 11, 60, 74
tension reduction, 1, 20–21
the Troubles, 33
This Country is Ours platform, 61–62, 66–68, 116
TKP (Communal Liberation Party), 61–62
Touval, Saadia, 18
transparency, 88, 127–28, 134
Treaty of Nice, 13–14
Trimble, David, 80, 84, 86, 92, 99, 102, 107–8
triple-lock system, 83
trust, 3, 13, 19, 28
Tunisia, 25
Tunisian Confederation of Industry, Trade and Handicrafts (UTICA), 25n3
Tunisian General Labour Union (UGTT), 25n3
Tunisian Human Rights League (LTDH), 25n3
Tunisian National Dialogue Quartet, 25n3
Tunisian Order of Lawyers, 25n3
Turkey, 35n1, 55
Turkish Cypriot Chamber of Commerce, 67
Turkish Cypriots: buffer zone and, 32, 43, 54, 59; EU accession and, 29, 35; minority status of, 32, 34; origins of conflict, 31–34, 59; *taksim* and, 31. *See also* Annan Plan (Cyprus); *specific political party or organization*
Turkish Cypriot Teachers Union (KTOS), 61
Turkish Republic of Northern Cyprus (TRNC), 32, 54, 63, 113–14. *See also* Annan Plan (Cyprus)
Tzionis, Tassos, 70–71

U2, 99
UBP (National Unity Party), 50, 66
UGTT (Tunisian General Labour Union), 25n3
Ukraine, 8
Ulster Defence Association/Ulster Freedom Fighters (UDA/UFF), 33
Ulster Democratic Party (UDP), 80–81
Ulster Unionist Party (UUP): agreement design and, 16–17, 120; campaign messaging, 99; civil society mobilization and, 101, 102; kin-states and, 109; Mitchell and, 85–87; political inclusion and, 89; power-sharing and, 80; release of paramilitary prisoners, 84, 86–87, 97; split in, 92, 95, 102, 107–8
Ulster Volunteer Force (UVF), 33, 80–81, 92
Union for the Total Independence of Angola (UNITA), 2n1
Unionist parties. *See specific party*

United Democrats (EDI), 50, 64, 68, 71, 72
United Kingdom: accession to EU, 35–36, 134–35; Brexit, 134–35; Cyprus and, 31, 55, 57, 59, 69–70; Northern Ireland and, 32–33, 81, 97, 120
United Kingdom Unionist Party (UKUP), 39, 80, 83, 89, 91–92, 102, 112–13
United Nations (UN), 2n1, 8–9, 19, 37–38. *See also* Annan, Kofi; Annan Plan (Cyprus)
United Nations Good Offices Mission, 50, 51, 58, 65, 70, 112, 125
United Nations Peacekeeping Force in Cyprus (UNFICYP), 31–32
United Nations Security Council, 51, 53n1, 57–58, 60, 64, 67
United States, 2n1, 7–8, 19, 35, 36, 57, 79, 130. *See also* Holbrooke, Richard; Mitchell, George
Uribe, Álvaro, 124

Vassiliou, George, 35, 51, 71
violence: agreement durability and, 3–4; bombings, 33–34, 79; cease-fires, 1–2, 32, 36, 79, 83; in Derry, 33; in East Timor, 8–9, 132; escalation of, 8–9; ethnonational conflict and, 2, 8–9; *frozen* conflict and, 43; in London, 79; media leaks and, 88; paramilitary, 33–34, 36, 43, 79, 81, 82, 90, 101; re-escalation of, 84, 129–30, 131, 132; in South Africa, 131; spoilers use of, 23; the Troubles, 33
voters and voting: agreement design and, 8–9, 16–17; alignment of, 10–11; education of, 28, 123, 127, 128–29, 133–35; effects of party splits on, 108; eligibility of, 30; Franklin's Theory and, 12–13; manipulation of, 8, 135; socioeconomic conditions of, 29; studies and surveys of, 16, 74–75, 106, 108; tools to influence, 11–12. *See also* public information; public opinion; public opinion polls
voter turnout, 29, 42, 85, 101, 124, 129

Wanis-St. John, Anthony, 130
Weitsman, P. A., 13
Western Sahara, 8
Weston, Thomas, 67
Women's Coalition. *See* Northern Ireland Women's Coalition (NIWC)

Zahar, Marie-Joëlle, 23–24
Zartman, William, 18
Zurich-London Agreements, 59

Joana Amaral is a research fellow at the Centre for Conflict Studies at the University of Marburg, Germany, and has a PhD in international relations from the University of Kent, United Kingdom. Her research focuses on the in-depth study of peace negotiations and mediation, particularly concerning issues of transparency, civic inclusion, and public engagement.